THE
PITTSBURGH
NEIGHBORHOOD
GUIDEBOOK

THE
PITTSBURGH
NEIGHBORHOOD
GUIDEBOOK

EDITED BY BEN GWIN

Belt Publishing

First Edition 2021
ISBN: 978-1-948742-71-9

Belt Publishing
5322 Fleet Avenue, Cleveland, Ohio 44105
www.beltpublishing.com

Book design by Meredith Pangrace
Cover by David Wilson

Contents

Contents

PART 3:
DOWNTOWN, NORTH, AND SOUTH

Contents

Introduction

One of my favorite views of Pittsburgh is driving out of the Fort Pitt Tunnel at night, when the downtown skyline appears out of darkness. Lit up and framed by yellow bridges, the city feels full of possibility.

"Possibility" is something of a watchword in much of the recent writing about Pittsburgh's supposed renaissance. Yet there is a disconnect between the stories of the normal people who live in Pittsburgh and the sponsored content extolling the city's revival. According to the latter, UPMC, Walnut Capital, the tech industry, and the Mayor are saving our city from the brink of a post-industrial hellscape. The reality is much more difficult and complex.

Like most of the country, Pittsburgh suffers from wealth inequality, gentrification, and racism. There's lead in the water, and we lack reliable public transportation and affordable housing. Development and redlining segregated the city decades ago, and those divisions remain. The police are militarized, and our schools are underfunded.

We started soliciting work for this collection in spring of 2019, and all the submissions were sent in before the coronavirus pandemic and George Floyd's death. But while there aren't direct accounts of the protests or sheltering in place, the problems plaguing Pittsburgh and other American cities that have been further exposed since March 2020 are evident in these stories. A feeling of unrest runs through much of this book.

Jason Vrabel and Brian Broome's essays directly address displacement and gentrification during our awkward in-between phase of urban renewal. Brittany Hailer and Jim Daniels write about addiction and the ongoing opioid epidemic. There are essays about work and family by Vince Guerrieri and Lori Jakiela. Bowie Rowan and Ed Simon write about mass shootings and the community's response.

There are more sentimental pieces, too. Multiple works mention of the fascinating steps to nowhere scattered along the hillsides. Stories of fistfights and heartbreak and hope set against a city with an identity crisis. I love baseball, so I am grateful to include Shannon Reed's story about our sad franchise and its beautiful ballpark. As a lifelong Pirates fan, walking across the Clemente Bridge to see Andrew McCutchen and the Pirates in a pennant chase after twenty years of losing was a surreal, fleeting experience that I cherish.

Also included in the anthology are essays and poems set in the surrounding towns and suburbs. The story of Pittsburgh would be incomplete without Braddock, Trafford, Penn Hills and others.

I read and accepted the work of many writers I didn't know before curating this guidebook. That was the best part of the editing experience. I am also pleased to include stories from a few dear friends and mentors. I hope the work in these pages paints a full picture of life in the region. And that it speaks to who we are as students, artists and workers in the Rust Belt and what it means to embody the region. There is more to our city than the downtrodden, Trump-supporting coal miner, and the transplant tech worker who complains about air quality. Pittsburgh is resilient.

I grew up in New Jersey, but my daughter has spent her whole life here. For her middle school writing class, she was assigned a neighborhood essay. She wrote about having two neighborhoods. She wrote about Evans City, where her mom and grandmother live. Riding her bike down the big hills to her friend's house, and going to the ice cream place in town. She wrote about our house in Bloomfield, playing catch in Friendship Park, her cat, and walking to the gas station on Liberty to get hot fries. She wrote about how great it was to live in the city and the country. Her mom died in July 2018, and the support we received from our community was humbling.

As my daughter has grown into a tough and compassionate teenager, she's embraced the city. We talk about different bus routes and the fastest ways to get places. We spend summers at her softball games around Pittsburgh. She and her classmates protest climate change and police brutality. My daughter's generation gives me hope, just as I'm hopeful that this wave of civil unrest can lead to systemic change. When in-person classes resume, my daughter will return to school downtown, between the bridges, with a view of the skyline.

PART 1

EAST PITTSBURGH

Swisshelm Park

CAMERON BARNET

It's easy to love what's easily missed:
If this elbow of the city could bend itself
open, loose with the weight of its history,
loose with the long wind of Commercial Street
like an umbilical cord, loose with Whipple Street
steep slopping into Edgewood, you might feel
the flex of the Monongahela passing by, a figure-8
of fancy homes, rows and rows of neighbors
like aisles passing over a petite plateau, the hum
of some distant freight moving through the night,
and you might feel the amenity afforded
by this place—the small delight of being forgotten.

It's easy to love what's easily missed:
the air raid siren wailing long into a new millennium,
a highway screaming by, a river sleuthing out
this semi-suburb, well known woods wrapping
themselves around the neck of the neighborhood,
my childhood bike doing loops around the low and long hills
of concrete, tire tracks of a third-generation boy
scraped into the blacktop, third iteration of integration
into Windermere Drive, home in the crook
of the road, home by an island in the road, island
sprouting a lone tree, the tree rising taller with
each generation, centuries seeded and ceded
by the Susquehannock and Iroquois, who take
no small delight of being forgotten.

It's easy to love what's easily missed:
the space between vale and helm razor thin
but deep cut by borough and court claim,
land divided and sold for summer homes
on the old farmland of Jane the abolitionist,

who taught and fought for women, who fed
and hid freedom-seeking people, the Underground
Railroad being the first trains to station here before
steel and slag and industry dusted over the sleepy
cul-de-sacs and dead ends—easy to love. Easy
to miss all the life you pass by on your commute,
all the history these congested tunnels plunge through,
all our small delights cooped and cupped up
in the bent arms of embrace—hard to be forgotten.

Solemn Pittsburgh Aubade

CAMERON BARNET

There are houses on fire every night here. It doesn't seem a sin
to let them burn. It doesn't scare me
to wake up to their ghosts still hanging skyward—a siren in the War
Streets, its doppelgänger spotted in Garfield
clear across the city tucked tight between smokestacks smacked
along every shore, barge-brown rivers
in a slow grind against the Allegheny plateau. Nothing much changes here.
It was built this way and it was built to burn—
I like it like that. After all, what is water without steel to cross it,
a mountain that you cannot pierce,
a city without forest all around? Here is where autumn comes to die
on stone steps and gridless, potholed streets.
I spend my days by a cathedral watching traffic swell and swirl. I spend
my time like a poem spends its lines
trying to find where to pause and where to stop. Most endings
and pauses I find can hurt. One time,
I loved somebody. One time, I crossed this street when I was in love.
Time will damage anything if you let it,
so we've built this place to last, placed placards of history along the streets,
and landmarked any building that dares to crumble.
This is Pittsburgh: black and gold bones buried deep, dinosaurs
at cobblestone intersections wrapped in scarves,
hundred-ton iron ladles frozen in shopping districts—we only fight each other
about what doesn't get to stay. Sometimes
on these stone steps, I fight myself about what to keep and what to remember.
My heart is a museum where all the exhibits
are closed. Love in this city comes as often as the sun, the reset of September
pulling clouds over Mount Washington
where I lived and worked, where some nights I'd walk its edge and see
houses burning on the horizon, and feel
the flames in my chest. I didn't have a word for it then. All I knew
was the feeling of coming home in the evening
to my roommate on his computer watching videos of chess masters

playing each other, the silence of him
slumped sideways on the sofa, stacks of Nietzsche and Jung casting shadows
on half-full-half-empty coffee cups, eyes heavy
with the shade of the room, a reflection of Bobby Fisher in his glasses,
hand on the rook and my roommate's hand
on the trackpad—history with the slide of a finger.

Paper House

CORINE DUVAL

I moved from Cleveland to Pittsburgh in 2006, eighteen years old and running from a life I could already see the end of. My father overdosed when I was four, and a single mom meant too much TV; Catholic school taught me to hold all my pain and turn it to shame; and then there was the grey city snow. When I was seventeen, and a man came to the house to yell at me about how my mom wasn't paying the mortgage, I was already halfway out the door. I finished high school living at a friend's house in the Tremont neighborhood, and my mom moved thirty miles west to live with my grandma in Medina.

I spent that summer saying goodbye to the city. I was reading the pleas of D.A. Levy before he committed suicide: "I don't want to die in Ohio anymore." I walked through the tunnel on the shores of lake Erie where they had found my friend Ben dead the year before. And I laughed with my friend Quincy at Edgewater Beach while we sang Tracy Chapman's "Fast Car." By the fall of 2006, I was ready to be done with Cleveland.

The move to Pittsburgh was easy. Like Cleveland, it had a legacy of industrial barbarism and palpable racism embodied in the pointillism of blighted buildings, food deserts, and lead in the water. But in Pittsburgh there was something new for me: possibilities. I had collected some friends who were all heading there from various points in the Midwest—Ohio, Illinois, Indiana. We migrated to the liminal spaces of the Steel City, and in those gaps I found a community that, for a while at least, made the burdens I came with seem insignificant.

In the urban fault lines we searched for new ways to live. Fifteen of us moved into two attached, abandoned row houses on a steep hill, and I lived there for two years. That was squat number one. For the next nine years I moved around Pittsburgh, squatting different houses—six in all—trying to find safety and a different life.

I never would have called it homelessness, if you'd asked; I had houses. You see, squatting is something else, somewhere between homeless and home, between choices and trapped. But the story I want to tell right now, the one that often feels the most important, begins in the middle with squat number four. It's about a boy and a house, but to tell it I have to go back to house number three, and a little of two.

Matt and I had met early in the summer of 2009, in a car full of friends leaving Pittsburgh. I told a joke he thought was funny, and so we fell in love. It was that easy. We parted ways in Denver, and when I returned a month later, he had moved to Pittsburgh and was living in a squat across town: number three. This home was so large that I never truly got to know all the banisters, landings, mantles, and halls. I never went to the basement, and never saw the backyard. The roof had caved in, or so I was told, but since it was summer and we only occupied the first and second floors, it was as remote as the future and of no great concern. I remember how white everything was: the walls, the rubble, and what was probably lead paint all over the hardwood floors.

I was still at squat number two, a story in its own right. But I would spend time at number three instead of my own place, conflating our new romance with the beautiful old house. Then I moved in and there were five of us: Matt, Flynn, Erin, Kelsey, and me, all living an absurd, quixotic life: for meals, we ate gummy vitamins we had stolen from Whole Foods, imprinting colorful stains on the white sheets (they never did wash out). We read a children's book aloud, and under the covers we passed the novel between us, feeling ourselves echoed in the orphans of Jorge Amado's Rio de Janeiro. In those brief moments we were a tableau of childhood dreams and the ache of adult nostalgia.

But all of this ended quickly; when number three was raided by the police after the G20 summit that summer, the blanched house was ripped apart, tagged and codified beyond all meaning. Flynn ended up in jail, and the menagerie of objects that made up our lives were called evidence. It was really only one month there for me, but in memory-time it is epic.

With Flynn in jail, Kelsey and Erin moved into apartments. That left Matt and me to find something new. Friends of ours squatting a house across town got jumped, and it scared them back to New England. They gifted me the squat before they left, so we moved in. It was up a steep hill—as are most of the squats in Pittsburgh—with city woods all around. To get there, you went up a crumbling set of cement stairs, pushing past tree of heaven and knotweed, until the house finally revealed itself all at once on the top step. It was a haven in the city, and more than perfect. It came with stolen electricity straight from the telephone wire outside, which was surely about to catch fire any moment. (Years later, it did.) There was no water however, so when we dirtied dishes we'd smash them ceremoniously in the backyard and steal new ones.

Matt and I had almost no possessions, but we filled the space quickly with everything we could find. If white paint is to be the defining memory of number three, paper of all color and make defines number four. We held the house together with paper—pamphlets, flyers, notes, and pieces. He formed a magazine, and we had a room full of partially working printers that hummed a mechanical symphony through the small house, spitting out reams of our polemics that piled on the floor.

We became lost in the archives of our own history. On good days, under blankets, we read and discussed Stirner, riots in Greece, bank robbers in Italy, all in whispers. On bad days we debated the nuances of love until his shouting and thrashing brought the house close to crumbling. Back then it seemed like we couldn't survive unless it was on the precipice of some great disaster. But we kept going, embedding ourselves in crisis and extremes. He broke the house apart with every emotional outburst. It was a bowling ball down the stairs, a kick through the railings, another broken door. We hid money above the ceiling tiles and stacked bats by the door. All the while the printers screamed a motorized dissonance and produced ever more copies.

I don't remember ever sleeping. At 3 a.m., Matt would kick the soccer ball loudly against the walls, paper flying—a remedy against writers' block as he tried to finish another article for that damned magazine. And me? I tried to keep it all together. I would organize my trinkets over and over, reexamining all the pieces of my life, and move stacks of paper from one box to another, trying to find meaning in the microstructures I could control. But I did not feel in control. Living in a whirlwind of paper, there never seemed time to ask about the things that were tearing us apart. Another copy, another forgery of another feeling. And the printers performed their final cacophony.

This could have been a love story, if he was a better man and it wasn't the Rust Belt. But I ended it—ended us—and he demanded the house. I could have fought for it. But what would I have been fighting for? Paper? Textualized plans and well-made arguments? No. I know we could have done it all so much better. All that possibility: windows to start, happiness to end. But I couldn't keep holding us both up when he was so determined on the fall.

I moved back to house number two for a time, Kelsey and Matt started dating, so she moved into number four. I heard their fights got so bad they were pointing guns at one another, but mostly I lost track of them. Word was they left when the mold and raccoons finally took over. And then the house was empty.

I returned once more to number four, before the city tore it down. Paper and shotgun shells covered the floors. The smell of mold was overpowering. On the walls, in red ink, someone had written: "Matt is an asshole", and that they "stole your shit." I appreciated the spectacle of it. I took a toy plastic Happy Days record player and some back issues of his magazine from the ground, and then I left for the last time.

What a mess: number four, a paper house full of drafts. They tore it down, like all the old places, four years ago. We never took a single picture, and I have made so many edits to the memories I no longer remember the original. But that empty lot on Pacific is where we lived for a time, and where I learned that safety can't come from hiding. And so I say, to the boy and to the city: "You were always an asshole, and I stole your shit."

Fanny at the Bingo

LORI JAKIELA

I worked bingo nights at the Trafford Polish Club Mondays and Wednesdays. I was seventeen and worked for my grandmother Ethel, who ran the kitchen. Ethel was 230 bad-tempered polka-loving pounds in a housedress and slippers.

"I don't need to impress anybody," Ethel said. "I don't gussy up."

I'd been working for Ethel since I was twelve. I liked the money for clothes and books and music. Ethel paid me what she felt like, depending, but there were tips and everything was cash, wads of ones that, on a good night, made me feel stripper-rich.

I could pocket bills, but a lot of the senior citizens at bingo tipped in change, and Ethel made me put the coins in a jar that she tallied every night. She called change-tips "found money." Found money, Ethel claimed, was lucky. She traded in the change for instant bingo tickets, the kind where you pull the paper flaps back to see if they spell out "Bingo" or the message, "Sorry You Are Not an Instant Winner."

We were supposed to split the tickets, though I don't remember every agreeing to that, and Ethel always took more than her share. She thought I didn't notice. I think she hit a few times but kept it secret. I'd win a dollar here or there, but never enough to make back what was in the jar.

"You weren't born lucky like me," Ethel told me more than once.

"We're family," Ethel said as she'd dole out my pay from her apron pocket. "And family is more important than money. Family is more important than anything. Remember that."

And so I didn't count my money in front of Ethel because it seemed disrespectful to do so. I didn't count it until I got home to my room, where I closed my door and spread it out on my bed and sorted it into piles and tried not to do the math when I knew my grandmother shorted me.

"Be grateful," Ethel said about everything. "You kids today are never satisfied. You're always looking for the easy way out."

I wasn't satisfied, but most days I worked hard for Ethel. I wanted her to love me. I was OK with the smell of grease and fish. I was used to Ethel's habit of eyeing up my boobs to see if they were growing. I was used to the way she'd make me turn left, then right, then left until she got a good look.

"You been letting boys play with those?" she'd say until I felt myself curl into my self like one of the ingrown toenails I'd clip for Ethel because she couldn't bend down to reach.

Safe sex, Ethel said, meant never letting a boy get on top of you. Safe sex, Ethel said, meant staying away from boys, period. Ethel seemed obsessed with talking about sex and had been like that long before I knew her. For years, my mother, Ethel's daughter, thought girls got pregnant if boys' tongues got into their mouths. My mother would grow up to become a nurse. My mother would believe in science. When I asked her how she ever bought the idea of spit sperm, she said, "Your grandmother is not someone to argue with."

"They're only out for one thing," Ethel said about boys.

Ethel said, "They can't keep it in their pants."

Ethel said, "That's how you happened, probably."

Ethel said, "You don't want to end up like her," meaning my birthmother, who'd been pregnant and alone and, as Ethel told it, a great source of shame for her family. My parents adopted me when I was one year old. Ethel loved shame as a weapon most of all.

I never knew Ethel's husband, my grandfather. He died the year before my parents adopted me. He was an orphan, too. I've seen pictures—a tall thin man with dark eyes. He looked sad in his suspenders and fedora. His orphan story was different—his mother dropped him off at an orphanage when he was 10 because she couldn't afford him anymore. No shame in that, Ethel said.

In pictures, my grandfather looked plowed over by the world, like Ethel gave him a go, too.

"Maybe he would have known what to make of you," Ethel would say.

She said, "I think he would have loved you.
"

———————————

It wouldn't occur to me until years later that my adoption might have been a problem for Ethel, who was old-school, a first generation American who believed in blood.

"Your mother couldn't have children of her own, so we got you," Ethel said about my arrival into her family.

I didn't read anything into that for a long time because I was used to

Ethel's gruffness, the way she hit me with the wooden spoon she kept near the stove, the way she'd try to chase me around the Polish Club kitchen and pull my long blonde hair. Sometimes I'd hit back. I'd joke about how I'd love to see her in a bikini, or about how many boys must have played with her boobs over the years because they were so big she could rest a tray table on them.

"Must be convenient on vacation," I said about her boob tray.

———————————

This is how it was between us.

Ethel was my only living grandparent and I had a lot invested in our relationship. I loved her and believed, in her way, she loved me back.

Or that she would love me back if I just worked harder, if I was a good granddaughter, if I complained less, if I made others happy, if I didn't fight so much.

"Lori baby."

She called me that.

———————————

Even a meteor of a woman like Ethel has a nemesis, or at least a foil. For Ethel, it was Fanny.

Next to my grandmother, Fanny looked like a toy person, something made of pipe cleaners and worn-out felt.

"Old Piss and Moan," Ethel called Fanny.

Every Wednesday, Fanny would come to bingo night and order her usual—fried fish sandwich, half a bun.

"And blot it good," Fanny would say, meaning she wanted the grease from the fish sopped with a paper towel before I served it to her.

"That Fanny gets my goat," Ethel would say, her face turning red as the roses on her housedress. "That Fanny can go to hell."

Why Ethel was so furious with Fanny, I didn't know. Maybe there was history there, maybe not. Whatever it was, neither woman ever talked to me about it.

"Let sleeping dogs die," my mother, who mixed her metaphors, said about the two of them.

———————————

Ethel and Fanny were neighbors. Ethel lived in a yellow house with two windows on the second floor and a white porch awning that made the house look like a duck. Fanny lived in a lopsided white box of a house that seemed about to collapse down the ragged little hill it was built on.

The houses, like the women themselves, seemed like something from cartoons. Ethel the fat spastic quacking duck, Fanny some sad thing a wolf started to blow down but gave up on because it wasn't worth the effort.

Ethel cranked up Frankie Yankovic's "Beer Barrel Polka" in the kitchen and laughed loud enough to flip gravity.

Fanny complained. About everything.

"That's noise pollution," Fanny said about Ethel's music.

"B-12 never comes up," Fanny said about the bingo. "They pump it full of lead so it don't float. They don't want me to win, that's why."

Fanny said about the fryer, "When is the last time you changed the grease?"

"Oh piss and moan and moan and piss," Ethel said. "Why don't you drop dead already?"

Every Wednesday when Fanny would show up, Ethel would say, "You again," and Fanny would glare.

"I don't know how you can stand her," Ethel would say to me about Fanny. She said it like a challenge, like she was testing something, loyalty maybe.

At seventeen, I didn't mind Fanny. I thought I knew something about sadness. I was drawn to it like a mirror.

Ethel believed in blood. I believed in bonds between strangers, my fellow oddballs. I romanticized every hurt, real or imagined. I read Vonnegut, who taught me both world-weariness and its opposite.

"Be kind, babies," Vonnegut said, his only advice about living.

I wasn't born kind, and most of the time I fought with everyone close to me, but kindness to strangers was easier. I practiced on people like Fanny and worked my way up, to my mother and Ethel. It didn't always go well.

"And so it goes," I'd say, Vonnegut's line, something to wield like a sigh.

I never thought about what it would feel like to be Fanny and know I was someone's test subject. I never thought about the difference between genuine and practiced kindness.

"You people are trying to kill me," Fanny said, and she meant Ethel and me and everyone else.

I don't know how old Fanny was but she seemed ancient. Her unhappiness carved her face and hands into canyons, things that take centuries to form. In all the time I knew her, she never smiled.

"Give me one thing to smile about," Fanny said.

I took it as a challenge. I'd tell Fanny a funny story from the news, some neighborhood gossip. I'd share the latest good-luck bingo trick I'd overheard, usually some new troll doll or a prayer to an obscure saint who specialized in bingo players and lost souls.

Lately I'd been seeing St. Expeditus around, on glass candles and necklaces. Sometimes he was brunette, sometimes blonde, sometimes bald with a silver bowl balanced on his head. No one was sure he'd ever been a real martyr. His backstory was fishy—Roman soldier martyred in Turkey, beheaded, set on fire, fed to lions, drowned. One story went, the devil came to Expeditus disguised as a crow and tried to delay the would-be saint's conversion to Christianity. The crow cawed "tomorrow, tomorrow" over and over until Expeditus, in a hurry to save his soul, shouted "today, today" and stomped the crow to death.

I told Fanny that story.

"They call him the Saint for Real-Time Solutions," I said. "Expeditus. Expedite. Clever."

I said, "He's the go-to guy if you're desperate."

I said, "You have to run something in the paper for it to work."

Fanny looked like she needed to spit. "Everybody has a gimmick."

About me, she said, "They see you coming."

I didn't know who she meant by "they."

Everybody, probably.

"Leave it be," my grandmother said. "That Fanny loves to hang on her cross."

Every Wednesday, Ethel would pretend Fanny wasn't standing in the Polish Hall kitchen, ragged wallet out, demanding Ethel serve her. Every Wednesday, Fanny would inch closer to Ethel, two planets bent on collision, until I put myself between them and took Fanny as my responsibility.

"All yours," Ethel would say when she saw Fanny coming.

My grandmother would bow a little and say, "Be my guest."

———————

One Wednesday, Fanny came in. Her dyed black hair curled like a raccoon on her head. Every week she seemed a little shorter and this day the top of her head hit where my boobs would have been if I had them, if boys really had been doing the job my grandmother believed they were born to do.

I had to stoop to look at Fanny. Her eyes, as usual, were red and runny, like she was allergic to the world and everyone in it, like she spent most of her downtime weeping.

But today there was something charged about her, too. She looked alive. She shifted from side to side, like she was revving up. She ordered her fish, half a bun. Then she added, "And you. Stop pussyfooting around."

She said, "You know I can't have the grease."

She said, "You people are trying to kill me."

I must have somehow botched the grease-blotting last time and Fanny thought I'd screwed her over. I was therefore responsible for a week's worth of burping and indigestion and all the unhappiness in Fanny's world.

Or it was more than that. It was probably more than that.

Here's the thing: I didn't know anything about Fanny's life. I didn't know if she'd ever been married, if she had kids, if she did have kids where were they and so on. I didn't know what music she may have liked beyond polka noise pollution, or what the inside of her sad little house looked like or if she had cereal in her cupboard or what toothpaste she used or if her teeth were mostly her own. She may have had doilies on her tables. Her house may have smelled like lemons. I didn't know and I didn't care, not really.

All I saw in Fanny was a generic sadness I thought I could connect to and fix. She made the world simpler that way. She made me feel useful. She offered me her sadness, my sadness; her outsider-ness to pair with my own.

St. Expeditus, help us.

St. Expeditus, get us the hell out of here.

People serve us in the way we need them to serve us.

By us, I mean me.

"I'm on it," I said about Fanny's fish, and turned back to the fryer.

Most days, I spent my downtime lying on my pink-shag bedroom rug, head wedged between two stereo speakers. I played Springsteen's "Darkness on the Edge of Town" over and over and pondered how to get out of Trafford, this rusted mill town with its Big Bang Bingo Jackpots and these fish sandwiches and a creek so polluted it turned everything it touched—rocks, tree roots, skin—orange.

Trafford—home to churches and funeral homes and dive bars with clever names like Warden's Bar and the Fiddle Inn.

"Get it?" my mother said. "You fiddle in and stumble out."

Trafford—home to my grandmother and my mother and Fanny and me.

"You're going to go deaf," my mother said when she found me lying with Springsteen like that.

She said, "Get up already and make yourself useful."

She said, "Don't you want to be somebody?"

I said, "Doesn't everybody?"

I said, to my mother who'd given up a nursing career to raise me, "And who did you want to be?"

"anyone lived in a pretty how town," e e cummings wrote.

"I'm nobody," Emily Dickinson wrote. "Who are you?"

"Temporary," people say about lives they're born into and plan to fix.

I wanted to be a writer. I wanted to go to New York and Paris. I wanted never to stumble out of The Fiddle Inn or work bingo night in Trafford ever again.

What I thought Fanny wanted:

To be somebody other somebodies would listen to and care about enough to give her food the way she liked it.

To believe her health mattered to someone, which meant her life mattered, too.

To believe that someone would notice some Wednesday if she didn't show up.

I took it on myself to be the person who would listen to and notice Fanny's presence and absence.

What I wanted: for my life matter a little, too.

———————

Sometimes I still think about my Uncle Milton, the retired banker, who died alone in his house in Braddock. I was young when he died, maybe ten or so. He was my dad's brother. I saw him at funerals, the occasional Christmas. He wore nice suits and smelled clean.

What I knew: Uncle Milton was a bachelor. He loved money and the stocks and had a subscription to the *Wall Street Journal*, which my father said was expensive and something only a jackass like Milton would spend money on.

Uncle Milton was dead for more than a week before anyone noticed. The newspapers piled up on his porch. The mailman called the police to check it out.

I'd been in Uncle Milton's house a few times. It was dark, the furniture heavy and expensive looking, the curtains heavy and expensive looking. A gold-framed picture of Jesus's sacred heart hung on the wall. In the picture, Jesus's chest was split open. He held his heart in one hand. The heart was on fire. The heart was crowned with thorns. His other hand made the sign of peace, two fingers together, pointing up.

"All that money and he dies alone like that," my father said about his brother.

"Do you know who you have in this world?" my father would ask, and most times he'd let the question hang like that, a blank to fill in, something obvious.

———————

"one day anyone died I guess," e e cummings said, "and no one stooped to kiss his face."

Vonnegut said, "And so it goes."

———————

If you want St. Expeditus's help, you must present him with an offering.

Pound cake, for instance.

Back at the fryer, I worked Fanny's fish as she stood by and watched.
I made a big deal out of lifting it from the hot grease and letting it drip. I put it on a paper plate and let it rest there a bit. I took paper towels, a wad of them. I blotted. I blotted again. I blotted again. I worked like a surgeon trying to stop the bleeding. I took my time because so much depended on me doing so.

Fanny watched. I could feel her watching. Over on the stove, a pot of hot dogs boiled down. I tried not to think of Fanny like that, withered and curling into herself, the smell of old hot dog water on her breath.

In the background, I could feel my grandmother watching too. I knew if I turned she would look disgusted. I knew she'd have her hands on her hips.

"Pain in my ass," she said under her breath, and then, louder, "That Fanny is a pain in mine."

I turned. I looked at her to say, come on, let it go. I looked at her to say, Fanny likes to hang on her cross let her hang.

This got my grandmother going. Her laugh bounced around the room like a bullet.

"Get it, Fanny?" she said. "You're a pain in my ass."

She said, "Fanny is a pain in mine."

Then my grandmother slapped her own huge ass and held a pose, The flesh underneath quaked. Fanny looked like she might cry.

"It's o.k.," I said. "It's done."

I hurried things up. I tucked the fish onto its bun and handed it over. Fanny inspected it. She pulled it close, then held it at arm's length, then close again.

"That's more like it," she said.

Then she tipped me a quarter.

This was 1982. A quarter could buy a phone call or some gum and Fanny could pretend she didn't know but she did.

I could tell by the way she gave it to me, like she was pinching my palm, like she hoped maybe the quarter would turn into a razor and make me bleed a little so I could know how it feels.

This made my grandmother laughed louder.

"Cheap is as cheap does," Ethel said as Fanny waddled off, holding the fish on the paper plate in front of her with both hands, like it was something holy, an offering on fire.

I put Fanny's quarter into Ethel's found money jar. I hoped maybe it would be lucky this time.

Saint Expedite, do this for me. Be quick.

As Fanny made her way out to the hall, I could hear her talking to everyone and to no one. She said no one knew how she suffered. She said she checked all her cards to make sure B-12 wasn't on them. She said she couldn't bear it. She said if she wasn't careful, the grease would keep her up all night.

She said it was about her heart, which of course it was.

Wilmerding, Pennsylvania: Thinking of Fred Voss

DAVE NEWMAN

The houses are being foreclosed on
but the kids are still in the streets
playing with chalk, riding bikes

and the old men sit outside a café
drinking coffee, waiting for the bars

and I am walking here
because I have been unemployed for two months
and what I can afford is the YMCA
to lift some weights or swim
then walk the cracked sidewalks outside

and I remember reading Fred Voss' poems
in my tiny apartment when I was 21 or 22
all those wonderful lines about working
as a machinist up and down the coast
of California and inside Goodstone Aircraft Company
that awful place with sparks flying and sharp objects
and bosses welded down to the meanest of hearts

and I remember thinking:
Jesus, I hope I don't end up like Fred.

How beautifully he wrote!
How hard he worked!

Fred dropped out of a PhD program
to become a machinist
but I was going to graduate school
so I didn't have to work with my hands,

probably my father's dream, a factory worker
who'd been employed since he'd quit
school in the sixth grade to load melons

but the directions drive us, not vice versa,
we end up where we end up, not where we want.

I wanted to teach college but no one liked my poems
about working as a janitor and taking drugs
and reading Nicanor Parra in the parking lot
before work with a ham sandwich in my lap
and my professors thought I was unintelligent,
not academic and/or a heroin addict, plus
I once showed up to party with a three-gallon
ball of beer and everyone else brought hummus

so I graduated in two years with a 3.8
and got a job in a warehouse
where I loaded ball-bearings into a truck
and delivered them to factories
and read more poems by Fred Voss
who was still a machinist
who is still a machinist
who is still writing poems

who is the only poet in America
who is the only poet in America

who could have survived in Wilmerding, Pennsylvania
circa 1870 when George Westinghouse
opened the Westinghouse Airbrake Company
and the men worked 55 hours a week
with steel made to stop a locomotive

and I like to think of Fred in the fire
burning with the men who had to burn
because he wanted to burn
because he knew someone needed to record this—

how practical poetry is in the hands of a machinist
how you can still build your life around poetry
when it's made by people who make things we need.

But it's 150 years after George Westinghouse
opened the Airbrake plant and the black smoke
looked like clouds and prosperity and now the city
is a shadow of itself, factories looking like
factories but not doing what factories do

and I have been reading Fred's poems again,
terrified and in awe, thankful and humbled

but this afternoon, it's 90 degrees
and I have my own work
my heart pumping past
the railroad line that hauls coal somewhere
away from Wilmerding, Pennsylvania
where Fred Voss never lived or worked
and a dog on a chain barks viciously
at a black torn garbage bag
and two guys covered with tattoos
head up a ladder, carrying shingles.

Frick Park

DAVE NEWMAN

A gray-haired man
stops walking his dog
to talk to another
gray-haired man
about
his second heart attack
both smoking cigars.

I Was Heading to the O on Forbes Avenue in Oakland

DAVE NEWMAN

which is the neighborhood where
the University of Pittsburgh is located

which is the school I attended that year
though the year before I attended

a community college and the year
before that another community college

and by attended I mean I sat
in classes and felt confused

while writing notes that sounded
like canaries in a coal mine.

My father worked in a factory
that made pick-up trucks.

My mother checked the hearing
of elementary school children.

In college I neither made
things nor provided care.

I took poetry classes and other
classes about rocks and dead presidents

and tried to imagine a future
while planning my death.

You can only fill a kid
with so much debt and anxiety

before they want to walk
the bridge to nothingness.

It was Friday night and I was drunk
with a bunch of friends, guys who

still attended community college
and/or worked bad jobs

and lived at home and hated
the humiliation of sleeping

in the same bed they'd slept in
since birth, all because of money.

Jobs looked like a treasure map
compared to college

and factories dying turned
the treasure map upside down.

We parked at a meter and climbed
from a dented and nicked Monte Carlo

and headed for the O
The Original Hotdog Shop

a greasy dive that served
French fries in paper boats

so large and overflowing
three people could eat themselves

sick on a large. Did they charge
extra for gravy and cheese? Yes

they did, so the world looked
terrible from almost every angle

even fun, even cheap eats
even our late-night stroll down Forbes.

Be warned: this poem ends
with cops and poetry, not fried potatoes.

I'd earned a C- the previous semester
in my Introduction to Poetry Class

or whatever the fuck it was called
but I adored the teacher, Toi Derricotte

a woman who talked a lot
about being black and from Detroit

which was confusing
because she looked white

and we were in Pittsburgh.
She referred to herself as light-skinned

and talked about her straight hair
and the rift those things caused

with dark-skinned black people
whose hair curled and kinked.

I'd never heard anyone say
light-skinned or dark-skinned

or anything about oppression
not related to money and the lack thereof.

The people I knew measured
their lives in bills and debt

which is a different kind of pain.
The people I knew had skin

that looked like they walked
through meat grinders for a living.

Toi once sang a Billie Holiday
song in the middle of class

like it was a lecture
and her voice vibrated

with so much feeling
with so much ache

I put my face in my hands
but casually so no one would see

me cry if I cried and I definitely
cried because art

because song, because poetry
because twice after class Toi asked

if I planned to kill myself
which I absolutely planned to do

but which I felt less like doing
in the presence of her voice

which sounded like a jazz song
a breath of concern and community.

Another thing she asked
with equal weight

was "Who do you read?" like books
might be the antidote to death.

I shrugged because the answer
was no one and the textbook

we used in class bored me
and sometimes the words rhymed.

The world outside never rhymed.
The world made its own music.

Three blocks from the O
straight down Forbes Avenue

sat a used bookstore.
It was mostly self-help paperbacks

arranged on folding card tables
like an abandoned city.

I walked there with purpose
because I wanted to be reading

because I'd finally been asked
who I was reading and now

I knew I should have been reading
and I wanted to read, desperately

like how those TV preachers
healed sinners with a touch.

I wanted to be saved.
I wanted to be a savior.

I dug into the poetry section
and it looked like hieroglyphics
or maybe books of poetry
because I'd never read, not poetry

not really, just the assignments
in class and at home I'd read

the Bible and devotionals
because I'd been forced

to attend church
and forced to read

church stuff which sounded
like fantasy, a man surviving

in a lions' den, another man
slaying thousands with the jaw

of a donkey, a one-hundred-year-old
woman giving birth to a child

but now I stood
in the poetry section, pulling

and replacing and trying to focus
and pulling and replacing

and I shit you not
I picked a book because

it was blurbed by Dear Abby
who was famous for offering

romantic and practical advice
in a nationally syndicated column

which read like a candle
lit by your great aunt with bad breath.

But back to Forbes Avenue and the O.
I was medium drunk but super hungry.

I think we'd been smoking dope.
Maybe it was more. Drugs answered

more questions than my classes
and cost a lot less than tuition.

It was late. Most of the city's drunks
had found mattresses or floors

but we walked with purpose
and I kept wondering if I had enough

moncy to afford cheese or gravy
because ketchup was great but nothing

as tasteful as cheese or gravy.
I would have built my life

around cheese and gravy
if I could have afforded it.

But money. But poetry.
But late night with no chicks.

Those were my three thoughts
as I walked up Forbes Avenue

lagging, dreaming my dreams
when this frat dude in a frat jacket

walking with his frat pals in frat jackets
planted his shoulder into my chest

so hard he spun me like a top
which forced me walk backwards

to keep from landing on my ass.
The frat guy said "You want

some of this?" and started
his own backstep, waving for me

to come on, his buddies taunting
in their frat guy ways

tugging on their frat guy jackets.
I turned to my buddies

who were almost to the O
oblivious to anything but munchies.

I really did not feel like fighting
which is how I'd been feeling

about college and studying and life:
the effort may not be worth the results.

The results appeared to be endless
student loan debt and a job

selling things no one wanted.
I knew a dude going house to house

begging people to buy windows.
I'd eventually end up selling

windows and driving truck
and painting houses and caring for the sick

but now the frat guy flipped me off
and stopped and took off his frat jacket

in a very dramatic way
almost a dance, a boxer in a ring

so I touched my pal Pat
and said "I'm gonna go

knock this guy out"
which sounded better than suicide

but maybe not as great
as learning the trade of poetry.

I didn't wait around for Pat's response
or to see if he even heard my voice.

I started back down Forbes Avenue
away from the O and further away

from the used bookstore where I'd bought
There Are Men Too Gentle to Live Among Wolves

based on Dear Abby's recommendation.
I'd read the book in one sitting and knew

it was terrible, like babbling sermon terrible
with lines like "But you, Maria, sacred whore

on the endless pavement of pain"
but I loved it any way, for the words

the way they lined up like trains
rolling down tracks to some distant light

just as I was rolling down Forbes Avenue
hoping for light, meaning victory.

The frat guy strutted and bobbed
and sang "Come on, big man."

So I came on, three big steps
and threw a roundhouse at his head

like I wanted to remake his face
with dents and blood, and it landed

and he dropped like he'd been meaning
to take a nap right there

on Forbes Avenue, the Cathedral of Learning
less than a block away

a building named after
the religion of education

but owned by a corporation
charging thousands to learn.

I took all my poetry classes
in the Cathedral of Learning

and I sometimes rocked
at my desk, filled with language

filled with desire to be something
I'd never known anyone to be.

A week after this, Toi Derricotte pulled
me aside after class and handed me a book.

A week after this, when I'd already read
There are Men too Gentle to Live Among Wolves

three or four more times, studying lines
like "I played God today! It was fun!"

which was straight-up puke
but which I wrapped around

my brain like rope I could climb
to somehow leave the world

of bad jobs and worse debt
and endless violence.

I believed in rope.
I always saw myself as climbing.

I always saw myself
as falling from every height.

When my mother said God
would come back and lift

the believers through the sky
and I knew I was not a believer

I made a plan to grab
the rope of my mom's legs

as she floated to Heaven
so that I too could find the glory

but my mom said God wouldn't allow
sinners to be pulled up by believers.

When Toi Derricotte handed me
a copy of *What Work Is*

a beautiful burgundy hardback
with a factory worker on the cover

a girl too young to be a factory worker
I thanked her profusely and walked

to the nearest lamp and sat
and the poems read like cars being assembled

and I knew everyone, every character
the firemen and waitresses and line workers.

I knew the factories.
I knew the uniforms and gloves

and the marks on the skins
of everyone who stepped into fire.

I wrote fifty poems that week
burning up the cross

where experience hangs with language
hangs with imagery, hangs with meaning

and, more importantly, one of the frat guy's
friends said, "What the fuck, man?"

alternatively staring at me then staring
at his pal stretched out on the pavement

then he tried to shove me and missed
and spun back and I punched him

and, more importantly, another frat guy
said, "What the fuck, man?"

and my friends showed up running
and started fighting with everyone

sort of like the Socs and the Greasers
in *The Outsiders*, a book I'd stolen

from the mall in 6th grade
and which my mom rolled

her eyes at, meaning: don't read that book
and meaning: the only book is the Bible.

The fighting on Forbes Avenue continued
so I heard punches landing

like balls in a catcher's mitt
like birds crashing into windows.

Then two cops appeared on foot
their uniforms blue as the ocean at night

and they started shouting
and they started shoving

and they wore hats
with badges above their brims.

I got frat-punched
but was too hyped to feel it.

The guy I knocked out
wobbled back up and stumbled

into a cop, accidentally but hard
and the cop grabbed him

in some sort of hold
a sort of mid-body choke

and the kid instinctively started to swing
and the cop clamped down

so he trapped the kid's arms
so they pointed skyward like kites

and his shirt was up
and his ribs were exposed

and the cop said "He went for my gun!"
and the other cop instantly started

banging his billyclub on the kid's ribs
and my pal Pat said "Run!"

and we all did, both groups.
I booked ass straight

for the Cathedral of Learning
which looked like a brick dick

shining spotlights from 50 floors
so I ducked right and sprinted

past the museum and the library
places I knew but didn't know

a world I wanted to explore
but not now, obviously

then hung another right, past
the home plate from old Forbes Field

and ended up on McKee Street
in my shitty college apartment

out of breath, out of beer
my friends stumbling in

all of us scared but maybe
exhilarated but mostly scared

of cops and jail
and of falling in the street.

Nobody said anything then someone
said "You see the cop beat that kid?"

We all nodded.
We saw exactly what we knew.

You want to see your life in miniature
take a close look a billyclub moving

at the speed of bees' wings
on some kid's ribs and spine.

For years after this I walked past
the library and the museum

and the room where the Pittsburgh Cultural Trust
hosts the Pittsburgh Arts & Lecture series

and I thought: how can I be a part of that?
The answer was, of course, I couldn't.

They didn't let people like me in.
They still don't. That's okay.

I read every single day.
I taught myself to write books.

79

BRIAN BROOME

The very last 79 East Hills bus leaves Wilkinsburg Station at exactly 12:15am on weeknights and I am usually the last one on it by the time it reaches Park Hill Drive where I live. Not many people walk my neighborhood after dark. It is usually me, having gotten off a late shift at work, and the irritated bus driver sitting in silence underneath the flickering fluorescent light that sucks up any real light, blanching everything until it is an odd shade of greenish blue. The street is dark apart from the headlights of the bus and the ramshackle houses are set a bit back from the road where trees overhang. It would be charming were it not so ugly; the houses crammed up against one another like brown teeth. Poor makes everything ugly. The both of us, the bus driver and I, are silently impatient to be back in our normally lit homes and can just about taste freedom. But, tonight, our quiet time is interrupted by a rumbling in the distance; a communal shouting that grows louder and louder as the bus creeps slowly up Park Hill Drive and when the noise reaches its peak, we were set upon by a horde of drunken children who come out of nowhere like native warriors shrieking out battle cries. Illuminated only by public chariot headlights; shouting and banging at the sides of the bus seemingly to attempt with all their energy to rock it off its wheels and overturn it with me and a terrified white man inside. He leans on the horn, but it does not deter them. As with most miscreants, it only serves to incite them and fuel the attack to a fever pitch. I can smell liquor through the bus walls and the scent of marijuana far more pungent than the usual dusting of it that always hangs in the air around these parts. I briefly wonder where their parents are as if that would do anything to stem the tide of this ocean of howling black, bloodthirsty faces bent on the wreaking of havoc; this insanity. I can only assume my death is imminent. The driver is now frantically fumbling for his radio as it crackles and sputters with the sounds of truncated words as he tries to explain what's happening to some incredulous and disembodied voice. And then, as quickly as it started, it is over. The whoops and hollers that proceeded the attack fade off into the distance. The excitement couldn't have lasted more than a minute or so, but felt like an eternity and he and I quietly creep up the road where the bus heaves a sigh of relief and spits me out.

We are both as silent as we'd started out. He just pulls away noisily leaving me alone under a streetlamp until I can hear crickets. Welcome to the East Hills neighborhood of Pittsburgh where we proudly display the Seven.

Gluttony

"For the drunkard and the glutton will come to poverty, and slumber will clothe them with rags." (Proverbs: 23:21)

If you offer me a drink, you'll almost immediately regret it. I can guarantee it. When I imbibe, it's an all-day affair and into the night until my body can't take anymore. I will vomit on my shoes and start all over again. I won't stop until someone pries the bottle from my hand and locks me up. I love alcohol and would bathe in it given half a chance. Were I to have my druthers, I would completely bypass the circuitous route of my mouth and inject it directly into my bloodstream so that it could perform its magical workings with even more expeditious mercy. In my fantasies, every vending machine is stocked with deliciously brown liquors and little baggies full of granular white goodies and there is one on every street corner. In short, I am an addict. I am the innocent victim of an extended adolescence and an arrested development. I have drunk and drugged so much so as not to remember my own name on some nights, wake up in agonizing pain and do it all again the next day and the next. I am a glutton for punishment. But, firstly and most importantly, a glutton for intoxicants of all kinds. This is why I live here.

A life lived in avoidance of reality is expensive and the East Hills falls perfectly within my price range. I am here because I have drank my opportunities in life. I have drank away a good job. I have drugged away my vacations, and I have snorted my future. I have filled myself to bursting with pharmaceutical delusion and my punishment for all that fun is to live here where all Seven of them are on display daily. I have sacrificed the privilege of living in the nicer neighborhoods in the city. I live where I can afford. But, unlike these people, I don't belong here. I am literate. I have merely and temporarily lost my way, but I will recover. This ghetto element around here would never understand that here is a mere transitory stop for me; a blip on my radar. This is why they don't talk to me. I have made no friends here because I am bound for greater things someday and they all know it. They can smell it on me. I live here only because it is what I can afford; not because I am part of this cannabis scented Bedlam where the residents talk about doing time in jail the way normal people discuss going to the grocery store.

The problem with being a glutton is that there is always a price to pay in the end. Dues. For me, the East Hills of Pittsburgh is dues.

Pride

"Pride goeth before destruction and a haughty spirit before a fall."
(Proverbs: 16:18)

I live at caruncle of the Eye of Horus. On a map, you can see how the streets Park Hill Drive and East Hills Drive form an almost perfect Eye of Horus; a noose. I stand at the corner every day waiting for the 79. It's a convolution bus that goes round and round the rim of the Eye of Horus over and over again ferrying miscreants from one meaningless errand to another. The public housing complex is situated right in the pupil. Whoever built them this time made sure to make them colorful. The units are painted purple and blue and red in some sort of attempt to make them cheerful but resulting in what looks to me like a dysfunctional Gingerbread Land sitting atop a hill. The 79 circles the perimeter all day long. Round and round all day so much like water in a toilet bowl that won't properly flush.

My shoe has a hole in the sole today. I have no umbrella and the rain has gotten into and has dampened my sock. As I look up from this minor annoyance, I notice that today, she is wearing red. She is the woman who shoots me scornful looks and drives a car that shines silver like new sixpence. It positively gleams. I don't know what kind of car it is, but it doesn't belong here. It should belong to a celebrity or someone that I was told I should aspire to be; like a doctor or a lawyer. Its luxury belongs to a woman who stops by to visit my neighbor a few times a week. She parks it right in front of the bus stop obstructing my access to its utilitarian comforts when it finally arrives and today, her vehicle smells of coconut air freshener and an expensive flower based perfume. She emerges haughty and well dressed and, as the door opens, the rhythmic thump from rap music that was muffled before, booms at top volume from her pimped out ride. She is in red a red dress and high heels. I smile at her, but no return smile is offered. Instead, she fixes me with elevator eyes that start at the top floor of my nappy hair and end at my now waterlogged basement of a shoe with the sock growing soggier and slimier by the second. She moves past me wordlessly and lofty throwing an expensive shawl over her shoulder in a grandiose motion. I am in no position to be acknowledged whatsoever. She greets my neighbor and they proceed with some sort of hushed business inside his home before she emerges triumphant to, once again, climb behind the wheel of her blinding blingwagon and speed off only to park its majesty in the ramshackle driveway of the ramshackle apartment that she lives in a mere five ramshackle houses up the road. She lives here too. It will never cease to amaze me what great pains people who live in this ghetto will go to in order to try to make it appear as if they don't live in this ghetto. The dilapidated home to fancy car ratio is unacceptable and the combined cost of sneakers and clothes people from this neighborhood buy could most likely settle the national debt with change left over.

The issue of Pride in the East Hills is one that is complicated. And money is utilized not for what it can do for you in reality; but for how it can make you look in the eyes of others and in your own deluded mind. The bill of goods that's been sold around here is thoroughly on display in the form if intricate hairdos whose upkeep make it impossible to pay electric bills on time and the ridiculously expensive bottles of liquor at the conveniently located liquors purveyor (right next to the Dollar Store) that eat into the grocery budget. It's the kind of liquor that the rappers drink. You are what you wear and drink and drive and I, with my soaking wet sock and rain-dripping forehead, will not fall prey to it. I won't live up to the stereotype and be trapped here in a state of perpetual adolescence. It's a modest life that is the key to success and I won't forget that. The issue of pride in this ghetto is the issue that keeps people struggling. One must learn to adjust to one's circumstances. If they would only learn how to live within their means, all things would be possible. I narrow my eyes and take solace in the fact that The Lady in Red's fancy car will be taken away from her one day owing to her irresponsibility. Repossessed. Someday, I will see her on the 79 and I'll just politely nod in such a way so that she knows that I know that I've recognized her fall from ersatz grace and that she should have known better. It is my humble and modest nature that will one day lift me out of this place. Slow and steady wins the race.

Sloth

"Through sloth the roof sinks in, and through indolence the house leaks." (Ecclesiastes 10:18)

My doorbell is ringing at 8am on a Sunday morning and, before I even open my eyes, I already know who it is. He will keep ringing it until I get up to answer, so it's best to just get it over with right now. My vision is blurry and my body is heavy with sleepiness. I throw on an old bathrobe and lumber down the stairs holding on to the railing for dear life before I close one eye to look through the peephole. Face distorted through the tiny funhouse mirror glass and eyes popped out and run through with blood red spider webs. Thin as a rail and swallowed up in dirty clothes. He is sorry and I can feel his shame through the door before I even open it and, when I do, the cold blast of stale, sickly sweet liquor smell almost knocks me over carried by the chilly morning wind.

"I am so sorry, sir."

As we stand there and I close my dirty bathrobe around my neck, I know that these are the words he'll lead with. Jody has never called me anything but "sir" even though he is easily a decade older than me. His eyes are wet either with the cold or with the sting of being hung-over. He is sorry, but he does not remember fully what happened last night; only the flashing of police lights in the wee hours and that men in blue uniforms came to his house. As we stand there, both shivering, I take the opportunity to refresh his memory of the previous evening. Jody, next door neighbor and indolent drunk.

I spent most of last evening on my knees in my bed banging on the wall that separates our bedrooms. The walls around here are rice paper and whatever your neighbor does on his side may as well be done right in front of you. But even if they were constructed from Kryptonite, you could still hear Jody's insanity clear as a cannon shot. Like me, Jody is a drunk although a far less responsible one. I work for a living. But, Jody cannot be bothered to take up such intrusions. The bottle requires all of his time and I take this opportunity to not invite him in, allow him to shiver on my doorstep and recount every detail of his antics since I've been unfortunate enough to come to this place. He braces for the onslaught; head bowed unable to meet my seething gaze. I am furious with lack of sleep and we've been here before.

Last night, Jody, you began your screaming through the walls at ghosts and, as you stand here in the clothes that you've been wearing for a week, I need to once again, fill in your memory as you cover your face and feign remorse. You are like every other no-good, do-nothing drunk in this neighborhood and, underneath it all, I can tell that you are perfectly healthy. Able-bodied. I tell him proudly that I was the one who called the police and he whimpers with shame and his voice cracks out an "I'm so sorry, sir."

The fact of the matter is that no one visits you and you have no family because you cannot be bothered to get your act together, Jody. Your life is just one long comfortable nap on the couch while your surroundings fall to pieces. I have seen you day in and day out sitting and staring into space in the driver's seat of that stationary junk heap you call a car all day long getting drunk and then I have to deal with the fallout. You shout at invisible phantoms all night long and, last night, you took the show on the road out to our shared courtyard screaming for all you're worth and punching at the air. Your awkward and drunken Jujitsu was on full display for a private audience of me at three o'clock in the morning. I watched you through the window performing your clumsy kicks into the stratosphere fighting and shouting at an invisible attacker and falling over backward. Your pathetic attempts to recover leaving you rolling around on your back like an overturned turtle. It was the most movement I've ever seen out of you, Jody. So, I called the police. They came again to laugh at you openly and try to coax you back into the house stumbling only for it to start up all over again twenty minutes later. I will call the police every time even though no one else around here seems to be willing to for some reason. But, I will call them. Every night.

He still has not met my eyes. When he finally opens his mouth to speak again, I am foolishly waiting to hear something new come from his lips. But, he just stammers and, in a voice as brittle as kindling mumbles out yet another "I'm so sorry, sir." His breath cuts through the cold and causes vomit to hitch in my throat and I can tell that he's already thinking about his precious liquor to smooth over the rough edges of my harsh words. He embodies the work ethic around here. He inebriates himself to the point of dementia and thinks that the world owes him something. This is who he screams at every night through the walls. I'm sure of it. He is fighting the world

Through sickeningly sweet liquor breath and a hung head, Jody tells me that he'll never do it again and turns slowly to walk, not to his house, but to his car through the snow. I tell him that he might want to look into getting a job. He walks to the weird purple vehicle and gets inside where he'll sit in lethargy all day long trying to change reality by looking at it through the bottom of a bottle. I have work in a few hours, so I march back upstairs triumphant to try to get some much deserved sleep. I will fail. Because, as Jody and I both know, there is truly no rest for the weary.

Envy

"I have seen the fool taking root, but suddenly I cursed his dwelling."
(Job: 5:3)

Community Crime Update: 10/4/2015 Burglary/Aggravated Assault: 2400 Block of Bracey Drive, 7:30am.

A 36-year-old female victim reported that a known suspect, S.D. Kelley,

37 of East Pittsburgh, broke into her house by forcing open the front door. The suspect then stole a frozen chicken. Then Ms. Kelley pulled out a knife and began swinging it at the victim like a woman possessed. Officers arrived on scene and detained Ms. Kelley who they found out in front of the residence shouting. The frozen chicken was located roosting in her purse. Kelley told officers that she and the victim were both romantically involved with the same man. While officers were attempting to get the full and ridiculous story from this ostensibly grown woman, a male, M. Henderson, 37, of East Hills, emerged from the residence and tried to interfere with the arrest. Mr. Henderson shoved Officer Pucci and then took a swing at Officer McManaway. Witnessing this, Officer Welling deployed his Taser shocking the shit out of M. Henderson which immediately stopped his assault. M. Henderson was then also taken into custody. Both suspects were then taken to the Allegheny County Jail. Ms. Kelley was charged with Burglary and Simple Assault while Mr. Henderson was charged with Obstructing the Administration of Law and Aggravated Assault. When queried, neighbors chalked this incident up to just another in the daily recurrence of supposedly grown women fighting for the attentions of a no account man, as romantic entanglement and drama are the only things that people with no education, no future and no prospects ever spend their time on. Jealous and possessive behavior is what passes for romantic love in poor neighborhoods. But, many people in the neighborhood remain confused as to why a person would retaliate against a romantic rival by breaking into her house and stealing a frozen chicken. All have dismissed the event as just another in a series of ghetto dramas that make the neighborhood look foolish on local television. One neighbor, (standing at the bus stop with a hole in his shoe and suffering from obvious sleep deprivation) who wished to remain anonymous, rolled his eyes at the news of another domestic occurrence citing that "It happens every day because these people around here have nothing better to do." At the time of this printing, the whereabouts of the frozen chicken are unknown.

Lust

"They have become callous and have given themselves up to sensuality, to practice every kind of impurity"
(Ephesians 4:19)

Never in all my born days have I seen so many little babies slung over the hips of young girls. Some of these girls have two, three and even four young babies in tow each one smaller than the next like Russian Nesting dolls; the baby girls with beads in their hair each one unique as a Tiffany Lamp. Little brown goslings trampling all in a row with their mother goose at the helm cursing up a blue streak on a cell phone at some unseen boyfather who is not there to defend himself. The children remind her of his failures and wrongdoings and variations on the word "fuck" are her favorite insults to scream at him on the 79 bus as the children look on drinking in every obscene word. No one can just skip adolescence. You have to go through it even if, through your own lasciviousness, you find yourself in the position of being a parent.

The girl on the 79 has children crawling all over her. She cannot be more than 17 and although they're vying for her attention, she refuses to put down her cellphone. Her ability to ignore them is almost trancelike as she giggles like a school girl texting and social media-ing and leaving them to their own devices to run around the bus like wild moles. They're screeching and not even the sound of the music in my headphones can drown them out. The only communication she has with them is to curse admonishing them for behavior that she will never properly correct. She is weary of them. She hates them. You can see it in her face. As the bus rumbles down a road filled with potholes, her children are unsecured; free to bounce around like gumballs and come back bloody. She cannot be bothered. When I catch her eye, I take the opportunity to shoot her a scornful look which she roundly ignores to go back to her cell phone. And, in that moment, it all becomes clear. She was also raised by a child.

The news that sex causes children has not yet reached the ghetto. The housing projects near my home are positively swarming with children. They run around loose and hang out on the streets until after dark. I see adolescent boys and girls left on their own to claw at each other's genitals clinging to one another on the bus with more passion that I've seen in adults. The boys roam the streets like hungry lions in search of prey and I see girls of a tender age dressing far more seductively than should ever be permitted all while their parents are busy down the street fighting over unfaithful boyfriends and frozen chickens. The carnality goes unchecked and always ends with swollen bellies and dead end futures.

The girl on the bus is joined by a friend who also has children in tow. They talk about boys. They talk about how they'd like to "get with" this one or that one and they talk about famous ones and they talk about the ones who have the nicest asses; the biggest dicks. Grown woman talk out of the mouths of girls. There are few things more powerful than adolescent lasciviousness. The boys talk dirty and in harsh words about things about which they hardly know. Unkind and sexist. All the working parts with none of the knowledge or common sense and neither will ever be passed to them until it's too late; until they're five babies in and hopeless. The girls giggle and talk about nonsense and one of their children plops himself in the seat next to me because he can. He is sticky with sugar. I smile at him and his mother calls him back to her angrily and shoots me another dirty look. He is her reward for being an adult. There is not much teaching to be done when you are 17 and your mother is 35, so I am not annoyed by this. Their morass will deepen and the pattern of sex and children will continue. Sex, that adult feeling in the hands of children. They don't know the ways of the world and now they're thrust into it whether they like it or not. They will begin to resent the children more as they get older for stealing their youth and their opportunities. And money; that is something that will never come, but will still be slightly less elusive than escape.

Greed

"But those who desire to be rich fall into temptation, into a snare, into many senseless and harmful desires that plunge people into ruin and destruction."
(Timothy 6:9)

I am standing beneath the bones of industry. All around me are workmen in fluorescent yellow vests and hardhats shouting instructions at each other as they erect beams and walls and heavy equipment roars and jackhammers. The autumn sky is littered with progress and I'm standing underneath it all noticing for the first time that everything around here is changing. I notice for the first time that the bodega where I bought my cigarettes from the shady Indian people is gone and the nuisance bar just up the street with the shady black people is gone and the people all around me have started to change complexion. They are working on East Liberty just above my head; changing it just outside my field of vision. The club that used to play hip-hop music is gone and the whole block has been spruced up with gourmet pizza shops and artisanal cocktail bars. The projects that used to be here are torn down and replaced by a shiny red and white shopping mecca and there are white people participating in a spin class in the building that used to house the shady Arabic bodega. I just stand there soaking it all in as if it suddenly just sprung up around me when a woman approaches and stands beside me. She says, as if we were just in the middle of a conversation,

"You know, they gonna move us all outta here, right?"

East Liberty, the neighborhood just down the street from the East Hills, is changing from the ghetto it once was. It's changing faster than I can keep up. It's changing just like Lawrenceville did before it and the people who live in my neighborhood have definitely noticed.

"They are going to move us out of here as soon as they need the space." she continues to no one in particular. "Further out until they can't see us."

I stand there with this darkly black skinned woman that I've never seen before in my life and we watch the transformation happening right before our eyes. I don't live here, but I don't tell her that. She's looking up at the construction of a newer, shinier place and making plans. I can see it in her eyes. She's wondering where she's going to go and, although I don't want to believe her, I know that she's right. She is the kind of old, diminutive black woman who is always right. She is someone who's seen this a thousand times before. I pretend to not know what she's talking about and we both just stare up silent at the harbingers of her imminent dismissal. We stand close enough to be lovers as her scarf flaps in the breeze and, after I've steeped in enough of her reality, I just turn on my heel and walk away leaving her standing there looking up and wondering what on Earth she's going to do.

No one can prosper without taking something and no one can prosper lavishly without taking lavishly. The word on the street in the East Hills is that "The White People Are Coming". It's just a matter of time. I've seen them with my own eyes. I've seen them in the morning in casual slacks and shirts surveying the neighborhood and measuring things. It's just a matter of time. It's never done in an obnoxious way. It's always under the guise of progress. It's done very subtly and those who live here know that we're on borrowed time. There are many things that poverty produces, but noble behavior is not one of them. It frustrates to the point of meanness and strains relationships to the breaking point. It causes inebriation to feel like a daily necessity and makes you hate your neighbor. But, this neighborhood is what we've got and we can't seem to find enough in common with one another to make it better. The only thing that we do have in common is greed. Greed is why we live up here and that does not escape our attention. The greed, however, is not our own. It is the greed of those who decide that they need more space, more gourmet coffee and more spin classes. The stories of noble, robust and hardworking poor people are cherry picked to make the rest of us feel worthless. These stories are romanticized versions of what poor actually looks like in America. Poverty and racism leave you feeling like less and cause you to behave like less out in the streets. It skews the priorities and, on some days, makes you so angry that you become confused as to where to aim it.

There is an angry hum over the East Hills neighborhood at night under flickering streetlamps when everything appears to be quiet. You can feel it. It causes random children to attack buses and early morning frozen chicken larceny. The anger is misdirected. We all know why we're here. It's because of someone else's greed. The greed of those whose toilets we scrub and security we guard for the promise of a better tomorrow that doesn't come. Someone has to do it and it may as well be us. Often, the quiet around here is split wide open by the sound of a gunshot. The relationship between the haves and the have-nots is anything but symbiotic and the anger around these parts is electric and alive and it has to go somewhere. So, we aim it at each other and we rarely ever miss.

Wrath

"Refrain from anger and turn from wrath; do not fret—it leads only to evil. For evil men will be cut off, but those who hope in the LORD will inherit the land."
(Psalm: 37:11)

The couch in my apartment is too close to the window. I'm thinking this while bathed in red and blue lights that always seem to turn my small dwelling into a perverted disco. I think that I don't want to be sitting here one day and catch a stray bullet while I'm watching something ridiculous on television. I giggle to myself as the lights dance around the room and I'm moving the couch thinking that the police would find me, bullet to the brain, mouth open in a frozen laugh as reruns of the old "Mary Tyler Moore Show" still crank out canned laughter from my television set. I move the couch because it just makes good sense to move the couch. I move the couch because wrath roams the neighborhood freely; less visible in the daytime but still fully present. When liquor and anger start to flow so does blood down the sidewalk. I try not to watch the news. I don't really need to because I can hear it all on the 79 the next day. So, I move the couch knowing full well that Mary Richards and the whole of the WJM-TV news team would never have to move their couches for such a reason. I laugh out loud again trying to picture Mary Tyler Moore's charming little apartment if it were plopped down in the ghetto. It's unfathomable. The next day, while running out to catch the 79, I stub my toe on the moved couch and when I board the vehicle, I limp to a seat.

The women sitting behind me didn't know her, but they knew of her. The woman who was murdered yesterday. They are speaking about her casually and not in the shushed tones that one might expect propriety dictates when talking about someone who was just murdered. They knew that he was no good; the one who killed her. He is only 20 years old and she was 28. She should have known better, they say. I put my headphones on and pretend not to listen, but I am listening intently to their judgment of the situation. They wonder aloud what her children are going to do. She had six of them and she should have been more focused on them than she was on a 20 year old man, they assess. And, as they speak of the dead in less than glowing terms, my whole body becomes heavy with the weight of it all. Six children left motherless. And, I have more than likely looked down upon this now dead woman on the 79 several times. I have probably watched her struggling with baby carriage, baby bottles and diaper bags and decided that her poor decisions have landed her here. But, I didn't want her to die.

The women behind me gossip on. Apparently, they argued about money, this murdered woman and her boyfriend. The lack of it, most likely and then they drank until 2am. They fought and then he killed her. And now I can fully picture the ghosts of the youth of her children sitting in the seat across from mine staring at me with eyes that ask me what I'm going to do beside sit here on the 79 looking down my nose at people every day. I have no answer for them other than I will move the couch. I move away from the window every time I see the lights conditioned like a Pavlovian dog. I wait for the news crews to go away every time someone is killed in the East Hills and then I emerge from my apartment like Punxsutawney Phil to cast judgment. There is murder and violence ever present around the Eye of Horus. It is the hum of anger that transforms itself to wrath that generates dead black bodies around here. Men, women and children murdered by their own on a shockingly regular basis. It's not just a news story when you live in the middle of it. It not just something to cluck your tongue at.

The women behind me judge on. They shift their own babies from knee to knee with the rocking of the 79 and they gossip. I don't want to hear them anymore. I turn on my music. It's the theme from *The Mary Tyler Moore Show*.

I once heard someone on the 79 say that, if everyone did the right thing all the time, there would be no one left to work for nothing. People from other neighborhoods look at us up here and assume that we are what's leftover and, on some level, we deserve to be here. Our bad decisions are what have led us to this place. But, if everyone made the right decisions all the time, there would be no one for everyone to look down on and it is in this way that capitalism works. We live here so that others can convince themselves that the worst of human instincts does not dwell in their neighborhoods. Only here. They can convince themselves that no lover's quarrel has ever ended in ridiculous behavior. They can convince themselves that no white child has ever done vandalism and they can convince themselves that "something like that" would never happen where they live. They can convince themselves that there has never been a drunk in their neighborhood who was in dire need of mental health care. We are zoo-ed and the chances of getting out are slim to none. They wonder aloud why society can't cast a play in hell and get angels for actors. They feature our awful behavior live every night on your local news before the blood on the sidewalks even dries. But, we're still here.

There was a time, long before my arrival, when the enormous, pockmarked parking lot across the street from my apartment was a shopping center. Now it is home to a single mega-church where people to go worship a Jesus who is never going to come for them. The only ones who are coming are the police who cruise the streets slowly day and night like sentinels.

Sometimes I wake up early in the morning with the sun and I find myself missing Jody. One night, the blue lights came, but this time they were cut through with red ones and I heard a lot of men talking outside and then they drove away in an ambulance and I haven't seen Jody since. New people moved in and told me that he died. He finally got out. It is at this time of the early morning that I know that I will not sleep. So, I go outside to stare out at the parking lot and wait for the sun long before the neighborhood wakes to put its two cents in and tell me who I am. I already know who I am and I'm not fooling anyone. I am not special. I am every bit a part of this neighborhood as those I complain about and like to pretend that I'm better than. I stare out at the empty mega church parking lot with the sun coming up all around me and I try to imagine what it must have been like a long time ago bustling with activity and commerce. But I can't really picture it.

I will be sitting on my hands and moving away from the window on cue when the red and blue lights burst through until they come to take the East Hills. And they will come and take it when they need more room. This, I believe is certain. We will never ban together to stop it and I'm just as guilty of inaction as anyone else up here in this ghetto. We hate each other up here. I'm not going anywhere. None of us are. Until the white people come to take it all away, this is all our powerlessness tells us that we can do until we are moved again and I will move right along with everyone else. And while I stand there feeling the sun's first morning warmth on my back, I can hear the 79 beginning its first circle of the morning at the caruncle of the Eye of Horus where it will go around and around and around all the livelong day.

Poem for Greenfield

KELLY LORRAINE ANDREWS

Praise the morning commute of 15 minutes or less,
the patches of meticulously mown lawns
and glass bottles of unpasteurized milk sold
at the corner coffee shop. Praise the Calvary
Catholic Cemetery, your preferred place
to walk and meditate—the awe of Mary's towering heart.
Praise the murmur of condolences heard
on Loretta Street, the long line of cars with
little white flags flapping from their hoods.
Praise the crossing guard who twirls his whistle
around his hand, carries dog treats in his pocket.
Praise the mirrors on barroom walls, the jukebox
with real vinyl records, ashtrays on every table.
Praise the duplex on Denmarsh where you led men
to an attic bedroom, traced the twelve meridians
inside windowless walls. Praise the alleyways
and tree roots bursting from sidewalks,
the hilltop views of yellowed bridges.
Praise the affordable one-bedroom apartments
with free laundry in the cobwebbed basements.
Praise Rialtos and their spinach, tomato, and feta pie.
Praise your past self who packed and unpacked
five times in eight years—sometimes to a street away.
Praise your current self for giving up the small-town
feel for pineapple curry in walking distance, Rocky's diner,
Saturday farmer's markets, the ice cream shop
and making coffee for your honey every day.
Praise Greenfield, your first made home,
and Bloomfield where you're learning
with your love how tall a coneflower can grow.

Bitter Melody

CEDRIC RUDOLPH

A sparrow hurtles from the sky,
clap of great oak's topple,
mottled beak-dollop
on sick-gray sidewalk.

Undone, bundle of nerves
and yarn.
Female, mother of six
living chicks.

Before her fall, she thatched
a nest in a crumbling wall:
straw, masticated newspaper.
Had just pecked seeds

from a feeder on Negley.
Wind wrapped cool around her wings
like a tiny bird-chemise.
Feathers, brown of desert rock.

Now her eyes crinkle,
the end of things.
Other sparrows twitch
and mourn. Ants

post home in her chest.
The colony needs a heart,
a liver, cells for the six-legged queen
stronger with scraps from above.

People will step over,
on, past the flat
skull and bones, never consider
the pipe-organ vocals,

the high notes she could reach,
bity soloist for willing ears,
her stage high in the eaves.

The Woman in Starbucks

CEDRIC RUDOLPH

The woman in Starbucks
mistakes me for a player.
I'm standing in line,
Thomas and Beulah under arm.
She asks, *What are you reading?*
Rita Dove, I say, *It's poetry.*
Oh, a poet, she says,
drawing out the *Ooooh*
and crinkling one stenciled eyebrow

as if I'm the kind of poet to fear, the kind of artist
who draws lovers in
like a trap-door spider,
as if I spend hours memorizing Etheridge Knight
or Langston Hughes
so I can rap smooth on street corners,
lead some fly honey back to my apartment
wallpapered in Dylan posters, Khalil Gibran
open haphazardly on a coffee table,

some tempestuous divo
more sullen than celibate
who can't hold a job past three months
and cries
like a curled shrimp on my duvet
while my boyfriend
swipes right on Grindr profiles.

No, I am not that type of poet,
I must inform her.
I just want to pass my grad school classes,
find a nice Pennsylvania boy to marry,
make enough money to buy

a bus pass and John Varvatos boots,
read enough books
to poach my eyes like eggs,
drink enough tea to stain
my insides purple.

Angel's Weekend

CEDRIC RUDOLPH

Angel plops on a stool
in Coffee Tree
reading "The Coora Flower"
from *Selected Poems: Gwendolyn Brooks*,
the book's splayed pages
obscuring half his boy-face

so absorbed in reading
if needed, he could not rescue
the overweight professor
if he chokes on a muffin.
He could not seal
the secretary's angry lips
before she turns,
curses her fiancé.

Angel spends most days
visiting libraries—Angelou's
Life Doesn't Frighten Me at All,
How to Grow Houseplants
topping the tower
of overdue books beside
the apartment door.

On Saturday, he hangs
at the yeshiva on Wightman,
trades a Yu-Gi-Oh deck
for one kid's yarmulke.

On Sunday,
guys on N. Highland Ave let him b-ball.
In their sweaty jerseys,
they don't mind Angel's onion-bulb wings

or that he reeks of myrrh.
He can pass quick, and lay-up.
He flits, just barely,
off the ground
for a jump shot,
scrunches his face,
flaps with all his muscle
to ascend to the rim.

Big Dirty's Pick Up Truck

MATTHEW WALLENSTEIN

He is big enough to break someone in half if he wanted to, but I have only seen Big Dirty hit another man in anger once and it was deserved. That's another story though. He is and has been by all accounts and experience what I consider to be a rare thing; a genuinely good person. He is large, kind, and can fix anything with a motor.

He bought the truck and loved it. This old rust colored Ford he got for transporting his dirt bike from place to place. The first time I saw it I was hanging out in front of Dave's garage in Braddock where Big Dirty, Dave, and Jay usually took turns fixing the clunkers I bought. Big Dirty was fixing some part of my car that he explained to me but I didn't understand. He said he wanted to show me his new truck and took me around the side of the building to see it. I was happy that he had bought it, it made him happy. He had had a rough go of it lately. He'd just split with his live-in girlfriend among other things. He showed me the inside, the outside, laughed when he said you didn't need a key to start it. He asked me what I thought about it, I told him I liked it, told him I used to have a truck, he asked what kind, I told him blue.

A couple days later, it was stolen for the first time. It was a blow to him. He had taken it to West Virginia once to ride his dirt bike, brought it back, and then one day when he showed up at Dave's garage where he had parked it was gone. Jay had borrowed it a couple times and he thought that may have been what happened. He made some calls and no one knew where it was. He caved and called the cops to say it was stolen.

Two days later, he got the call saying it was in an impound lot a couple towns over. The cop explained it'd been taken by some 15-year-old kid. They had pulled him over in McKeesport, he told them he was on his way to his girlfriend's house and he had borrowed the truck from a friend. So Big Dirty drove his dirt bike over to the impound lot, paid his $220, and got the truck back. There was a broken off key in the ignition belonging to a different vehicle that he had to fish out. When he turned it on, he found the radio cranked all the way up on a pop country station. The kid must have stolen it and turned all the way it up listening to Tim McGraw. He told me later the kid must have pried the old-fashioned smokers' windows open and gotten in that way.

When Big Dirty got it back to the shop he boxed it in to insure it couldn't be stolen again. He parked it right up against the building and had a car parked on each side of it. About a week later he showed up to work at Dave's around 8 in the morning and found a big empty space where his truck had been. The car that he'd parked behind it was sitting in the middle of the road. He just stood there a minute looking before an older man who was sitting on a nearby porch gestured to him. Dirty went over.

"I seen what happened."

"You did? You saw what they did to my truck?"

"About three, four in the morning, they come up in a minivan, a whole bunch of them get out. They get around that car and there was enough of them, they picked it up and moved it to the middle of the street right there and the one kid, he just got in that truck and drove away, scrawny kid, red head maybe. I would have called somebody but I was smoking a joint, I didn't want to get myself in trouble."

Dirty reported it stolen again. And he put the word out to friends that it was missing. He got a phone call, it was from his ex-girlfriend's new boyfriend of all people, telling him he found the truck. Big Dirty went over to where he'd said it was. It had been crashed, blunt wrappers were on the seat and floor, the door was open, the battery was dead. Jay brought him a battery and when they hooked it up the radio was on full blast again playing pop country. Same kid.

When Big Dirty got the truck back to Dave's he unplugged the battery and took it inside, He removed the starter, he unplugged the distributer. If the kid was going to try again it would be impossible for him to take the truck without those parts.

Dave installed cameras on his garage. For a few days things were back to normal. Then Dirty showed up to work one morning to find the hood on the truck with a battery and a distributer cable plugged in. If the kid had a starter Dirty would have been out of a truck again. I walked my dog down to the garage and they showed me the security footage. It showed a red headed teenager looking around, popping the hood, trying the set up, then leaving. He didn't look like much to me. In high school I probably would have beaten him up and taken his shoes.

Later that week Jay was making small talk with the guy who ran the junk yard across the street. He asked the guy if anyone had ever tried stealing a car out of there. As it turned out the junk yard had dealt with the same kid who took Big Dirty's truck. Apparently he had come by there a few times doing damage to things, breaking into cars. Most recently he had climbed the fence, broken into a car and driven it right through the fence to get out. He told him this time he had caused around 20 grand worth of damage. The junk yard man explained that, as it turned out, the kids uncle was a cop, which is why he kept getting let go without any consequences. But according to him he had had enough. He knew who the kid was so he found out where he lived, dragged him out of the house bear footed and scared the hell out of him, convinced him to tell the police the truth. His uncle got the charges down but couldn't make them disappear. He ended up with an ankle bracelet, but according to the junk yard man the last anyone knew the kid had cut it off and left town.

Big Dirty eventually sold the truck for what would have been a good profit if you don't factor in the cost of the impound lot, and towing, the cops, the wasted time, the frustration and all the rest of it.

PART 2

AROUND LAWRENCEVILLE, GARFIELD, AND SQUIRREL HILL

The Bride of Penn Ave

ALONA WILLIAMS

After *The Bride of Penn Ave* by Judy Penzer & Jill Watson

She the prettiest thing in this neighborhood anymore. The Bride of Penn Ave. Coming home after her wedding to find her friends and family waiting with eye watering food she can't eat until she has changed out of her dress.

Oak tree tinted chicken, dewy grass greens, potato salad clouds, daisy macaroni, marigold yams. Laid out like button downs on an ironing board.

Her mother meets her at the door. Groom not far behind. Smiles are the backdrop. Love is the celebration. I wonder if they have honeymoon kids. And if she can still fit her dress.

The Bride of Penn Ave married the Groom of Penn Ave and they had three children of Penn Ave. Been here from penny candy to dollar honey buns.

Hopscotchin on Graham.
Skateboarding on Kincaid.
Taggin stop signs way before the [redacted] came.

The story of the Bride of Penn Ave is a never-ending lineage
of Brides on Penn Avenue who have children of Penn Ave.

She is me. Before I was. Her fulfilled prophecy.

Place is the narrator here.

I could never just walk past her.
How many of you just walk past her?

Lawrenceville's Doo-Dah Days Are Over

JASON VRABEL

Strange Conditions
Family Day in the St. Francis Hospital outpatient ward was like Alcoholics Anonymous except run by a psychiatrist. The ward treated patients dually diagnosed with depression and alcoholism—like my mom. I'd been to AA meetings with her before, but Family Day was a first. After thirty minutes I was thrown out.

If there were signs pointing me toward outside, I didn't see them, and by the time I gulped outdoor air, I was a molten and disembodied blob of anger—the subject of a Francis Bacon tryptic: *Man in Elevator, Man Mistaking Gift Shop for Exit, Man in Revolving Door.*

Man? Barely, but unknowingly becoming one faster than I wanted to. For a twenty-year-old in a state of hot plasticity, something's bound to make an impression, an indelible imprint.

My family lived in a faraway suburb, so the streets of Lawrenceville were new to me, but I found what I needed, coffee at Wendy's and shade from July's late afternoon sun. With the hospital's brick wall releasing the day's heat into my back, I stared at the houses across the street. In each gable was wood trim shaped like a crucifix.

I'd soon forget these houses and everything that just happened, not thinking I'd return to this place, let alone build a life here. A place where I'd learn how to be a husband, father, and neighbor; where I'd become a witness to—and a participant in—the displacement of neighbors who previously built lives here.

The Shack Across the Street
In 2004, my wife, Heather, and I bought our first house across the street from a crater—a block long excavation site for the soon-to-be Children's Hospital of Pittsburgh—and next to it, a wooden shack. Each morning, head of security Sgt. Leonard Thomas emerged from it in uniform, dark blue pants and starchy white shirt, standing with his hands on his hips and legs shoulder-width apart. "Morning, Captain!" he'd bellow, a cigarette hanging from his mouth.

Lenny, as I came to know him, was a sixty-something black man who loved to gab ("Hey, Cap! Let me ask you something!"). I stopped by on my way home most days; at night, from my window I'd look for cigarette smoke drifting through cracks in the plywood shack and head over.

When Heather traveled, it seemed like I talked to Lenny more than anyone else. He wanted to remarry and move to Arizona, where his daughter lived. I sometimes wondered about the home Lenny returned to after spending so many hours in a tiny shack. He eventually did remarry, and at the reception at his Northside house, we sipped potent alcoholic Kool-Aid from plastic cups in the shade of an ancient oak, looking across the five vacant lots he turned into a sprawling grassy estate bordering a wooded hillside. I was too stunned to respond when Lenny spread his arms and exclaimed, "What do you think, Cap?"

Back at the shack, Lenny said, "Things are changing around here. Won't recognize this place in a few years. Just you watch." Unconvinced, I crossed the street for home, noticing peeling paint on our gable thirty feet above the sidewalk, yet another home repair I'd need to make. Only then did I see the crucifix-shaped wood trim. My knees buckled.

I knew all along that St. Francis Hospital once occupied the crater across the street, but I had long ago sealed away any memories of being in it. The seven years since my mother died suddenly felt like seconds as I looked across to see my 20-year-old self, looking back.

During the nineteenth century, St. Francis primarily housed the mentally ill. In fact, a square drawn on an 1883 map is labeled "The Insane Department." Later recognized as one of the best facilities in the region for those with mental illness and addiction, St. Francis treated patients from afar, like my mother; and from Lawrenceville, like our neighbor, a white lady I'll call Mary.

While walking her little white dog, Mary sometimes rang our doorbell to ask for water. Peering at the hospital's steel skeleton rising from the ground, she said more than once, "It's a shame, ain't it?" It was now difficult for her to get to the Northside for treatment for schizophrenia, she said.

Mary's building went up in flames in the middle of the night. By morning, the windows were blown out, the facade was charred, and Mary's dog was dead.

Mary had started the fire to dispel demons.

Pioneering

Heather and I were among Lawrenceville's "early" gentrifiers. Low on the gentrification pecking order, early gentrifiers proclaim ignorance about the direction their neighborhood is headed when they move in, then blame "late" gentrifiers for all that comes after—an advantage in the gentrification blame game.

Lawrenceville was more racially diverse than the city as a whole, but still predominantly white and working class, and its century-old brick row houses were aging fast. Crumbling mortar, sagging roofs, and economical repairs like glass block windows and painted brick facades were symptomatic of families losing their footing in a changing economy. Early gentrifiers, seduced by the authentic, raggedy charm of urban deterioration, heard the siren song.

Heather and I earnestly assimilated. In her bid for Democratic Committeewoman, Heather was trounced by the incumbent, a lifelong resident, but earned respect for trying. I repaired neighbors' leaky faucets and blown fuses, shoveled sidewalks, mowed lawns, and advised our octogenarian neighbor about refinancing her house after she gambled away her money at the casino.

Not long after moving in, while drunk on dollar Miller Lites and gambling at the "whiskey wheel" at the St. Augustine Parish summer festival down the street, I didn't hear the gunshots that killed a young man waiting at the bus stop a block away. No else seemed to either. The killers and victim were black. Later that summer, a white woman was strangled by a white man in the middle of the same street on a weekday afternoon (but survived). We stopped taking notice of raids by police, DEA, and ATF.

Lawrenceville became the place Heather and I called home for longer than anywhere since childhood. Our love for the neighborhood deepened after the birth of our daughter gave us new reasons to rediscover much of what we'd taken for granted. Its spectacular Allegheny Cemetery became our park; its riverfront gave our toddler the joyous *kerplunk!* of rocks tossed from the shore beneath the 40th Street Bridge.

Within walking distance were friends, restaurants, groceries, and bus lines with door-to-door service to the Children's Museum, aviary, zoo and other first-class cultural institutions. Lawrenceville began to feel like *Mister Rogers' Neighborhood.* While parenthood opens one's eyes, it also creates tunnel vision—our neighborhood was changing in ways we didn't grasp until it was too late. Lawrenceville was becoming exclusive and most of our neighbors would soon be gone.

In 2017, *Money* magazine named Lawrenceville the "coolest" neighborhood in America, and many other national publications followed. Since 2011, the neighborhood's non-white population has dropped by about five percent, and households earning more than $150,000 have increased from approximately three percent to twelve percent. Today, our 15201 ZIP code boasts the second highest 10-year return on real estate investments in the country (one of only two over 2000 percent). Lenny was right. Lawrenceville was a wounded animal with vultures circling overhead.

Confronting One's Own

Self-identifying as a gentrifier is less an act of falling on one's sword than of swallowing it. Fellow gentrifiers don't like it; often they prefer to mix a batter of merit and luck that, when fully baked, tastes strongly of achievement. Neither do the have-nots, who rightfully have little patience for any buyer's remorse that comes with privilege.

Naming oneself a gentrifier solves nothing, but neither does housing policy, it seems. However, instead of playing pin-the-gentrification-tail on some other donkey, acknowledging one's place in the cycle allows us to see more clearly the paths we've followed, and possibly become more than mere observers.

As one of eleven children, my dad's brother is fond of saying, "We had the one thing money can't buy: *poverty*." My uncle is free from that mill town poverty now, and though I've heard it many times, it wasn't until recently I sensed bitterness hiding in his jokey delivery.

My family lived at the lower rung of an affluent white suburb. When duct tape no longer held together our 1970 Plymouth Duster, we replaced it with an evolving array of Buick and Ford lemons. White skin helped my family escape poverty in only one generation, and buying a house that would appreciate in value was the keystone that held up everything else. It gave us something to borrow against for my out-of-state college tuition, and plugged an otherwise leaky bucket. Homeownership is the basis for Wealth-building 101, a class I was able to opt-out of.

Someday my wife and I will sell our house for a sizable profit which, beyond sweat equity and the actual dollars we've invested, will be unearned. What should we do with it?

We could avoid it by selling it to Lawrenceville's community land trust, a program that creates permanently affordable homes. But will that make any difference in a neighborhood now overrun by investors and flippers who are here solely for unearned income? Or do we stay the course and see our unearned income as our daughter's future college tuition, and keep the wheel of luck and privilege turning?

Gentrifiers' collective actions shape urban places in incontrovertible ways. Our mere existence in cities is problematic for lower-income people, yet our spending patterns generate revenues cities need to survive. We exacerbate others' pre-existing conditions and then pay for Band-aids. I often wonder if we should leave the city entirely. But for what? To raise another child who sees the world through suburban glasses? By age eight, our daughter not only knew what gentrification was, but had marched in the streets against it.

Unlike her, I didn't have any childhood black friends. Pittsburgh's suburbs seemed whiter then than now (which is hard to believe); despite living a mile from the city line, there weren't any black children to befriend. White people talking about having (or not having) black friends sounds absurd and maybe racist, so instead I'll talk about my grandma's black friends. To say she had them is an understatement; she *only* had black friends.

My maternal grandma lived in a public housing, where I spent many Sunday afternoons sitting in an open-air corridor on the thirteenth floor eating butterscotch candy and watching trains, usually with her and Miss Gray. From their East Allegheny neighborhood (now rebranded Deutschtown), they'd take me to Isaly's for ice cream, or on a bus to G. C. Murphy so that Miss Gray could buy 45 rpm records for me, including Devo's "Whip It" and Survivor's "Eye of the Tiger".

I'm not searching for some contrast to my white-and-in-the-vicinity-of-affluence upbringing. The black people of my childhood were all adults, and those like Miss Gray and my dad's co-workers helped me see beyond my township. Suburbanites have seemingly infinite choices available to them, including where to live as adults. Most return to their original homogenous, segregated nest; others, who see no chance for diversity in that nest, leave.

In the cigarette haze-filled rooms of the Viking Motel, my ten-year-old eyes were further opened to race, but also class. While my dad's black and white union brothers and sisters argued bitterly over wages and benefits during contract negotiations, I cut bologna sandwiches into triangles and passed them around. Only later would I understand that these workers were united against a common foe: Management.

President Reagan's systematic dismemberment of labor and dismantling of America's working class would eventually be felt from suburbs like mine to neighborhoods like Lawrenceville, where the seeds were sown for today's so-called meritocracy and the one-percenters, a class to which many of Lawrenceville's newest residents belong. By the time my Heather and I arrived, those seeds had sprouted and the working class was doomed.

Absurdistburgh

For some, Lawrenceville is a success story nestled within the even bigger success story of a city once dubbed "Shitsburgh" by film actor Sienna Miller, star of *The Mysteries of Pittsburgh*. Miller's no urbanist, and her opinion of Pittsburgh, borne from crankiness and boredom, would've been meaningless had it not been shared by so many of us. Had she not cut straight through all the talk of resiliency, resurgence, and our reinvention as an "Eds and Meds" city. Had she not hit that raw nerve in those of us who at some point succumbed to Pittsburgh's postindustrial malaise and thought, *Yeah, I'm from Shitsburgh.*

In the eyes of many, these are distant memories erased by Pittsburgh's triumphant return to the national stage as a center for autonomous vehicle research and other tech centric enterprises. But those eyes overwhelmingly belong to white people.

Following the 2010 census, Pittsburgh was the nineteenth most racially segregated city in America. Today, by most measures, it's also the least equitable, according to a recent report by the city's Gender Equity Commission and the University of Pittsburgh entitled, "Pittsburgh's Inequality across Gender and Race."

The report's co-author, Junia Howell, Ph.D., says that if black residents moved to nearly any other city, "Their life expectancy would go up, their income would go up, their educational opportunities for their children would go up as well as their employment."

This seemed like a long-overdue step in the right direction. But not for long. Soon after, a group of black women (with degrees in medicine, social work and other disciplines) penned a letter to the City that revealed the commission's research team to be overwhelming white, and noted that much of the content and many of the conclusions had already been established by black researchers who were excluded from the study.

One person who could have left but didn't is Damon Young, whose recent memoir, *What Doesn't Kill You Makes You Blacker*, belongs alongside August Wilson's plays and John Edgar Wideman's novels in their shared multi-generational depictions of being black in Pittsburgh. I can't recall being shaken by anything literary more than I was by Wideman's *Dumballah*, especially where he describes two men in Pittsburgh's Homewood neighborhood burying a dead infant in frozen ground. *What Doesn't Kill You* shook me too.

It's not Young's acrobatic writing that makes his book a high-wire act; it's his courageous, sometimes brutal, often hilarious, portrayal of the absurdities black Pittsburghers face daily. Young says he didn't write the book for white people, and while I understand what he means, I felt like it was, in fact, written *for me*. It's easy to admit that Young's humor made me laugh, sometimes uncontrollably, sometimes uncomfortably; but I'd be a lying fool to omit that I cried too, sometimes knowing why, sometimes not.

Young's first person accounts of the racial and class collisions redefining Pittsburgh today are more acute than anyone's. Comparing primarily black communities with mostly white ones, Young writes, "The main difference between kids from Wilkinsburg and kids from Fox Chapel or Mt. Lebanon...is that Wilkinsburg kids didn't have the privilege of making mistakes."

I agree. I'm from Mt. Lebanon and got to make a lot of mistakes.

The Gender and Equity's Commission's executive director, Anupama Jain, Ph.D., wrote that the report "is notable for remedying research gaps that occur when gender and race lenses are not used to assess the equity challenges confronting our cities."

This gap-remedying report about race and gender with major race and gender gaps seems to be the latest example of the absurdity Young describes.

Lawrenceville would be Pittsburgh's wealthiest neighborhood if most of its residents weren't dead, or so goes a long-running joke. Its population of about 12,000 residents jumps to nearly 145,000 if we count those buried in Allegheny Cemetery. Most of its headstones are modest, some unreadable after a hundred Pittsburgh winters. Many are opulent monuments—replicas of French cathedrals, granite obelisks, even a temple guarded by female sphinxes.

I've wandered through its pastoral 300 acres enough that Allegheny Cemetery feels like an actual neighborhood—not only the city's wealthiest, but its most integrated. Resting here are black judges, white industrialists, Negro League ball players, politicians, philanthropists, abolitionists, Civil Rights activists and Spanish Flu victims. Even Union and Confederate soldiers forever remain side by side. Most recent burials are members of black families from nearby neighborhoods. What does this say about "Pittsburgh for All," the slogan for a city that desegregates in death, but not in life?

The Education of Mister Rogers

The outsize influence of the made-in-Pittsburgh *Mister Rogers' Neighborhood* television show is not surprising considering a typical kid learned enough from Fred Rogers to earn a BA in Neighborliness. Paradoxically, Rogers' teachings were as easy to learn as children as to unlearn as adults.

In a seminal scene, Rogers invites Officer Clemmons (played by opera singer Dr. François Clemmons) to share a foot bath—bold for TV in 1969. As a young black man during the sixties, whose relationship with police had been marked by brutality, Clemmons said in an interview he was reluctant to play a cop. The unscripted scene moved Clemmons, yet he remained unconvinced his character could have a positive influence on "the real neighborhood," but later said, "I think I was proven wrong." If Rogers and Clemmons were courageous as hell—and they were—then what is Pittsburgh today?

Rogers' overarching lessons about being human haven't always come easy for me, but his more specific and repeated messages of inclusivity and being a good neighbor have.

Until now. Gentrification, as an issue, has raised my ire for two decades, but seeing it up close has made me spiteful towards newcomers, even though I'm a *beneficiary* of the property values they propel upward. Unlike many Lawrenceville long-timers, these newcomers have progressive bona fides—they put *Feel the Bern* stickers on their bumpers, recycling on the curb, and immigrant-welcoming placards in their windows that look out into a neighborhood that recently lost every last one of its 300 Somali Bantu residents. Yet I struggle with their lack of eye contact and refusal to utter hello when passing on the sidewalk, their social media whining, their entitlement to conflict-free urban living, their excessive wealth (and festoon lighting).

It's here that Fred Rogers challenges me the hardest. I think about Cathy, an investor who bought our neighbor's house and then attempted to extort $20,000 from my family when we sought a zoning variance. Could I share a foot bath with her? Why is my hostility bubbling up just thinking about it? Why is the ethos I ascribed to her then—a greedy parasite devoid of basic decency—hard to shake, despite our victory over her in a *property* dispute? Why do I still feel like our property rights were *earned*, and hers simply purchased? How did I come to see myself as being *entitled* to hold opinions about who belongs and who doesn't?

Rogers of course would not see me as hypocritical or petty, but would see that I see it in myself. He'd pause long enough for it to sink in; long enough for me to forgive all the vultures; long enough for me to forgive myself.

To tell you I've learned this lesson would make for a nice ending to this essay and notable milestone in my Lawrenceville journey, twenty-six years and counting, marked by death, birth, conflict and discovery.

But a dishonest one. I'm just not there yet.

Naming myself a gentrifier doesn't mean I've accepted that, when neighbors said long ago they felt threatened by new people coming into the neighborhood, they were talking about people like me. Or that my quality of life is now threatened in the same way. Or that this is, for the foreseeable future, irreversible.

This leaves me wishing for some other ending, like a Rapture that leaves behind only those who have been here a while. Or to write my own ending, in which I disappear into Allegheny Cemetery and *my* Neighborhood of Make-Believe. Will you join me?

Won't You be My Neighbor

Late at night, Gus Greenlee, owner of the Pittsburgh Crawfords Negro League baseball team, and Josh Gibson, a catcher regarded as the league's Babe Ruth, drift up a wooded hillside to a private mausoleum. Inside is Richard Mellon Scaife, former conservative philanthropist, tycoon and owner of Pittsburgh's Tribune Review. *Standing between its fluted columns and under a classical pediment, Greenlee knocks on a metal and glass door.*

"Mr. Scaife? It's me, Gus."

"Gus who?" Scaife growls.

"You know damn well Gus-who!"

"What do you want?"

"I need a newspaper man. Robert Vann's buried across town, so you'll have to do."

"Really? I'm remembered as a...newspaper man?"

"No, don't be ridiculous. It's Halloween. *Día de muertos!*"

"Oh no, not that again! Get off my lawn!"

"I have Josh Gibson with me," Greenlee says. "He'll drag you out if he has to."

Scaife rises like smoke from an ashtray, dusts off his suit coat and straightens his bow tie. "Same big feast as last year?"

"We're doing something *different* this time," Greenlee says. "Start waking the others while I run over to Section 21. I need a word with Stephen Foster."

Greenlee returns with the shaken musician to the ghosts gathered beneath a cherry tree by Scaife's grave. "Good to see you again, Stephen!" Scaife says. "What are you opening with tonight? *Camptown ladies sing this song! Doo-dah! Doo—.*"

"No!" Foster cries, glancing uneasily at Gibson's Louisville Slugger.

"No doo-dah."

Greenlee smiles. "I think we'll *all* enjoy what Steve has in store for us tonight."

The ghosts follow Greenlee, descending into the valley like fog, as Foster begins to play the Ink Spots' "Don't Get Around Much Anymore." Passing the Soldiers' Tomb, hundreds of uniformed souls rise, singing, *Missed the Saturday dance...Heard they crowded the floor —.*

On nearby Butler Street, Asher Newhouse stirs his old-fashioned at a picnic table outside North Park Lounge as his friends await his big decision. Meanwhile, a writer (and aspiring essayist) leaves Butterwood bakery and heads west on his bike.

A thousand more ghosts relieved of Spanish Flu join in. *Couldn't bear it without you-u-u. Don't get around much anymore —.*

To his corporate Uber co workers sitting beside him, Asher says, "Uber has been really good to me. My career has really taken off."

The writer (and aspiring essayist) nears Allegheny Cemetery. *Don't get around much anymore!*

"Smashing!" Scaife rejoices. The souls hoot and clap, momentarily pulling both Asher's and the writer's eyes into the distance. "I've got a tune everyone knows!" Scaife says. *It's...a....beautiful day in this neighborhood —.*

"But Google made an offer!" a recomposed Asher shouts over the clamor to his Google friends sitting across the table.

*A beautiful day for a neighbor—*sing one hundred thousand ghosts passing through the cemetery's stone gatehouse. *Would you be mine? Could you be mine—.*

Asher says, "I've decided —."

The souls crossing Butler Street swallow up the writer (and aspiring essayist) and his riderless bike careens into a Rover. *I have always wanted to have a neighbor, just like you—.*

Again Asher looks off into the darkness. "Do you hear that?"

Asher's pupils swallow his irises as hundreds of fingers reach through the patio fence, snapping its wooden slats. Boards are ripped away and in their place appears the smiling face of a ghost (and aspiring essayist), singing,

I've always wanted to live in a neighborhood, with you, so...

Sweat, Nails, My Father's Ladder

MIKE GOOD

When I climb the wooden stairs, run my fingers
along the palm-stained flaxen walls
I think of nails in the attic.
I feel broken nails squeezing through
shingles and purlins, bearing down my father's back
as he twists toward the whole house filter
in the corner of the crawlspace. I see cuticles
lined with midnight grease. I see the tips
of white rose petals. I see rafters weighted
with precipitation holding the weight of autumn
cutting into summer. I remember 1999. I feel the insulation
filling my lungs. I see the invisible things that kill us.
I watch razor nails bursting through oakwood and trees
swallowing hooks holding tire swings. I think I am dancing.
I think I am dancing across Yiayia's mustard carpet
in that split level in Millvale, and I think of all the houses
built with post-war swagger, built with post-war hope,
built across the places where hope never landed
and I think of the luck of it all: I think of the luck
of being alive, crawdadding across those six by fours,
doing that Mediterranean dance so as not to fall through the ceiling.

Steel and Glass in Margaritaville

MIKE GOOD

Blue does not convey the color of the sky
on a clear night in Millvale. Beside the Allegheny,
Pittsburgh pools into greasy silhouettes. Buildings descend
into water—the banker's green M, the steel tower
a grim charcoal prism, the blue neon needle of health shining,
crooked, and gashed. Raising glasses, we drink
together the way we have been drinking together
since we were sixteen. Between the Fortieth Street Bridge,
there is us, and everything between us. Now twenty-six,
working the same tired jobs again: the broken nonprofits,
the idiot bosses, the reckless wander, grinning
like the curve of this shit-eating river. A cover band
begins to play Jimmy Buffet—the patio brimming
with flip-flops, polos, and sundresses
shouting and loving and spitting through the air. The IPAs
have become sours. A train rings out. Summer
already ended. I am too loud. Then I am too quiet.
I am too drunk. I am too everything but here
in Millvale, where my grandmother lived, a block
from the fire hall she used to sweep. My mind dances
through, bubbles bursting in glass, memories
like buildings in water. You must know this, have
heard this a thousand times as you tell me
to quiet down. But now the city is gone. You are gone.
I am gone. Jimmy fucking Buffet is still here.

for Dean

originally published in *december magazine*

The Hour of the Cockerel

MIKE GOOD

Which is to say dusk is approaching,
as Pablo from Thessaloniki and Paige from Fox Chapel
prepare to say their goodbyes. Pablo moving back to Cologne,
which is a Latin word for *colony*. Paige back to Shadyside,
which is a Pittsburgh word for *nice place to live*. Tonight,
they stand on a rooftop in East Liberty,
the roof appearing not far from collapse, and all
around the old redbrick apartment,
new lofts paneled with aluminum rise.
Shall we mourn for old Pittsburgh? For the belching
smokestacks, the cheap pierogis, the rust
taste of Iron City? When Primanti's was a place to grab
drunkfood and on no blogger's *eat-before-you-die* list? Pittsburgh:
the unlivable, the vacant, the uninspired waste. Shall we mourn
this sunset, with Pablo and Paige,
shading the pale hotels atop North Oakland,
pouring crimson over the great green crown
of the Hill District? The sky is on fire. There is a certain light
in Pittsburgh that still causes me to salivate, a certain
blue that cuts inside the burning afternoon, that pulls one foot
in front of the other, a certain wonder
that lies in finding two strangers atop this old building,
drinking the evening. Maybe, they are in love, will find
each other across the Atlantic, or perhaps, in understanding,
will part. Sometimes it is more than one should expect: this paradise,
gazing from a roof, watching, releasing the caps
of Coronas with the lip of an old steampipe, talking of Athens,
peregrines, and change. Endless change.

originally published in *Salamander*

Lawrenceville 1996

LISA KIRCHER

In love with G
I was supposed to be her boss
So it was Mike who stayed up all night

He witnessed the dawn of my nervous breakdown
Lost every time I tried to find him in Lawrenceville
Always finding Lucky's in the Strip when I went out with Kora
(except when I took home that stripper and his cigarette left a mark on my
leather jacket)
In an attempt to simulate festive,
I wore my 1930s-era beaded pearl top to Hambone's, and laughed at
everything Potter said
G making up words to songs
Blackout drunk at the Warhol's opening party, the one we organized

Waking up with my face between her legs
Tressa, laughing, saying she liked me because I was shallow
I couldn't tell her about the seven years of sobriety I had before we met
Wondering if Jeff and I would still be together, another secret
Fearing no one would ever love me like he did
Thinking I'd never hear from his mom again
Knowing now that I was right, and Jeff is still dead
I can't remember when, exactly, but it was the year I had my last drink.

And how it turned out
No two loves are alike,
Not if you're trying.

Locks of Love

JIM DANIELS

On the Schenley Park bridge loaded
with padlocks clicked onto railings
(like Paris, but not), a kid with acne welts
red with fury wields a hacksaw yanked from
a Lowe's shopping bag that blows up and
over the suicide fence into Panther Hollow.

Near the center, locks hang clustered
in mad combinations or keyless like his.
Tough angle for sawing. Light drizzle,
gray March. I pause, my own lock clicked
onto the fence near the civilized library side
of the bridge—not the park's unruly sprouting

closer to him. Shirt-back black with rain
and sweat. When it finally breaks free,
he yanks it off, tosses it over the fence
like love's last hand grenade, then collapses
into his bent arm against the fence
shaking with moans and tears.

The bridge's fences were latched onto
ornate railings to protect impulsive students
from four nearby colleges after a series
of unfortunate leaps over the low railing
that also dragged a bald chemistry professor
to his death in their wake. Undertow.

The historical preservationists saved one
of three bridges over the hollow for jumpers.
I steer clear of that one, its gorgeous tug.
My lock celebrates 30 years of marriage.

You won't see me sawing it off. It could be
almost any lock now—the Sharpie not sharp

enough, our initials faded to rust. He can't be
the first or last to take a saw to one. They should
rent hacksaws at a kiosk on the corner. My wife
spotted a body one Sunday morning in the hollow.
She dropped the donuts she was bringing
home for breakfast. Seeing that kid's mad toss,

I'm glad the fence curves inward above the ornate
railing, its tiny wire rectangles too small
for footholds. I once shed mad teenage tears,
no bridge in sight, just a handful of pills.
Flat mid-Michigan mitten open in shame.
Young man alone with sorrow, imagining grief

when it was just an early storm. Locks of Love.
My daughter cut her long hair and sent it in
for cancer kids, then never cut it short again.
Pure innocent belief has its own brief scent.
Hacksaw or scissors—one way or another,
it falls free. My wife survived cancer. We don't

march in the annual Race over these bridges.
We'll all cross over soon enough.
We threw our keys over the bridge
with the others. Keys and dead bodies
down there. How many of you
remember your first combination?

The young man wipes his arm across
his face and looks up—catches my eye
on the other side. I pretend to look away
at my narrowing future, or back at
the confidence with which I said forever.
He tosses the saw over too.

August Pause

JIM DANIELS

to watch a young couple kiss in the street—
once, twice, pushing hard into each other
against a blue Kia with Ohio plates. Then
he slams the door. She stands on the curb
wobbling. He pulls away slow. She's moving
into Next Door, Pittsburgh. I sit on my porch,
happy watching dead ants fall from my roof
where the exterminator sprayed. At the university
where I teach, she'll get oriented this week—
that's the plan. What's their plan? Goodbye kisses
like that—young sugar kills an old man like me,
doubting their love can survive the distance. Poison
you can't see or plan for. Raining ants out here.

Hawk, Panther Hollow

JIM DANIELS

Too young, he insists, for this,
striding silent across the bridge
beneath a circling hawk
into the park. His tattooed arms

glisten August sweat—piercings
and his wallet chain. Thick black boots
dent soft grass. More than a costume,
he insists, more than temporary sinking.

More than the piercing of veins
he presently has no money for.
The panic of blurred desire, rocks
sinking smoothly to the river bottom,

unreachable as sky. He throws his phone
into a dented dumpster full of rinds,
chicken bones—flies rise briefly,
then settle. He didn't remove his battery

to disconnect his line to outer space.
He thrashes off a weedy path into brush.
Three death calls in a month, three friends
lost reception forever. Tears drip

into morning dew, though summer trees,
confident in their green, offer no comfort.
No one can find him on sonar or radar,
call forwarding or call waiting,

yet somewhere someone else was dead.
The hawk. The hawk can find him.

Squirrel Hill

ED SIMON

An *eruv* is normally a thin line of metal wire that stretches across the tops of telephone poles, barely visible to an observer who doesn't expect it, looking scarcely different from the normal infrastructure that you would see in any large city—perhaps a line to bring cable television into homes. But the purpose of an eruv is different; rather it serves to encompass a Jewish community entirely within a symbolic border, whereby private and public domains are blurred and it becomes possible for Orthodox Jews to carry whatever needs to be carried outside of their literal homes on both the Sabbath and Yom Kippur, the Day of Atonement.

In Pittsburgh the eruv encircles almost the entire historically Jewish neighborhood of Squirrel Hill, as well as Greenfield, parts of Regent Square, and Point Breeze, where I grew up. It runs down Forbes Ave, past verdant Frick Park and the Victorian mausoleums of Homewood Cemetery; through porched homes on South Braddock Avenue, and along the edge of the Parkway East; it briefly runs parallel to the meandering, brown Monongahela River, and snakes up Browns Hill Road; to the west it briefly dips into Schenley Park past college students playing frisbee or sunbathing (depending on the season); and it traces back around Wilkins Avenue. This thin wisp of ephemeral wire turns what is public into a common treasury— it converts an entire community into a home. More than that it functions as a membrane, as a skin; binding neighbors together as one body. A few hours ago, somebody whose name doesn't deserve to be mentioned pierced that skin, walking into the Tree of Life Synagogue on Wilkins Avenue with an assault rifle, and killing at least eleven congregants there to celebrate a bris. I still don't know who among the dead that I might know.

One of the largest urban Jewish neighborhoods outside of the New York metropolitan area, the community is home to dozens of synagogues across the entire theological spectrum, from small Hasidic shuls to massive Reform temples; from liberal Reconstructionist communities to modern Orthodox congregations. One of the city's largest and most diverse neighborhoods it's always been a haven for immigrants, from the burgeoning communities of Chinese, Korean, and Vietnamese who have opened up restaurants and shops which line Forbes Avenue and the long crooked, cement-cracked spine of Murray Avenue, to middle eastern immigrants who in the years before Pittsburgh's Muslim community would grow large enough to support halal markets, would do their grocery shopping at Kosher Mart.

Bordering both Carnegie Mellon University and the University of Pittsburgh, the neighborhood has always been an intellectual's paradise, the sort of place where homes are stuffed with an ungodly number of books and where the Carnegie Library is among the most frequented in the entire commonwealth. Squirrel Hill tolerates idiosyncrasy, uniqueness, oddness. Wandering the blocks of the central business district are scores of characters, dreamers, and schemers, scores of delightfully weird and open people. This was the location of the Presbyterian Church that Mr. Rogers, an ordained minister, would preach at. This is where Hasidic families walking to shul on Saturdays wish each other a "Gut Shabbos," something that owes more to Crown Heights then it does to the Midwest. Squirrel Hill is exemplary of America, of the best of the country. Which is why as our nation cannibalizes itself in a nightmare of fascistic hatred, it was the locus of this evil act.

Such is the continual nightmare of this American bloodletting, this "American carnage," these horrific, dark, exhausting, terrible, hellish atrocities visited upon our communities every single day. Too many of you reading already know what it is like to see your towns, your neighborhoods, your cities profiled on television and the internet after such hell has been visited upon it; too many of you know the surrealism of seeing those places which you love suddenly plastered across media because of the actions of evil men. And many of you who do not understand it inevitably will someday, and for that I am heartbroken. And for that I am angry.

That Jews were the target of this person's delusional rage is not surprising, at least not to anyone who has paid attention to both the vagaries of history and the hateful rhetoric which permeates our discourse right now. This is not an issue of "civility," or of "Both sides are responsible." No, I feel completely entitled to examine the poisonous fruit of our current political culture, and to rightfully accuse those whom now occupy the highest positions of power and influence in our nation, and to point to them as being those who are responsible for sowing such discord. Every antisemitic dog whistle, every hateful meme, every manipulative conspiracy theory promulgated by the current administration leads a path to what happened in Squirrel Hill today. But that man who occupies the White House, that thing who can't even utter condolences without blaming the victims whose blood is still warm—*that man does not deserve to have every single story be about him.* So content in knowing his responsibility, I will not mention him again here.

Because Pittsburgh—*Pittsburgh is blessed.* And Squirrel Hill—*Squirrel Hill is blessed.* So today, we say a *baruch* for Pittsburgh, for Squirrel Hill. We think of hanging out with friends in the dwindling twilight of a June evening on Forbes Avenue, eating Italian ice and seeing the sun reflected off the tops of distant skyscrapers. We think of the winding, cobble-stone streets snaking up the hill, and we think of mighty sand-colored synagogues which dwell at their tops as if golems surveying their villages. We think of pastrami at Rhoda's, pancakes at Pamela's, cheesesteaks at Uncle Sam's, cheesecake at Gullifty's, pizza at Mineo's, midnight breakfast buffet at Eat n' Park, and Iron City at the Squirrel Cage. We think of the boys in their black hats and the girls in their long skirts trailing behind them as they walk to yeshiva. We think of the Hebrew letters on the clock set in its tower at the JCC looking over the intersection of Forbes and Murray, and we think of creased used paperbacks by I.B. Singer and Joseph Roth purchased at Amazing Books or Classic Lines. We think of the triumph in vinyl in the rows of Jerry's Records, and we think of Christmas Chinese food dinners at How Lee or Chengdu. We say kaddish for those we lost; for wives and husbands; for sisters and brothers; for mothers and fathers; for daughters and sons. For friends. But we need not say kaddish for Squirrel Hill, for she is still there.

Squirrel Hill will always be my home, and my heart will always be in Squirrel Hill. When I was a teenager, my friends and I used to hang out "upstreet" on Forbes and Murray after school ended, incongruously grabbing cheesesteaks as Shabbos would begin in the early descending sunsets of winter. There was a period when we took to wishing each other a "Gut Shabbos" on those Friday afternoons, and though Judaism was not a tradition in which I was raised I was irresistibly drawn to this ritual, not just because of the sense of community which it offered, but in the mystical apprehension that the Sabbath could be as a world unto itself, a utopia of not space, but of time. In much medieval Jewish poetry, the Sabbath is presented as a Queen, who ushers in a brief kingdom that is as respite from the horror of this world. The modernist poet Hayim Nahman Bialik, in imitation of those Hebrew, Yiddish, and Ladino lyrics, wrote in a poem that the "sun has already disappeared beyond the treetops, /Come let us go and welcome the Sabbath Queen, /She is already descending among us, holy and blessed, /And with her are angels, a host of peace and rest."

Today I think of a different poem, by Pittsburgh and Squirrel Hill's native son the great Gerald Stern, who in his lyric "The Dancing" records his family's reaction to the end of the Second World War. He writes that he never "heard Ravel's 'Bolero' the way I did/in 1945 in that tiny living room/on Beechwood Boulevard" (which intersects Shady Avenue only a block away from Tree of Life). Stern writes that he never "danced as I did/then…doing the dance/of old Ukraine" for "the world at last a meadow, / the three of us whirling and singing, the three of us/screaming and falling, as if we were dying, /as if we could never stop" here "in Pittsburgh, beautiful filthy Pittsburgh." The wisdom of "The Dancing" is the wisdom of the Sabbath, that even in the midst of such pain, sorrow, heartbreak, and evil, there is still the respite of that sacred day, when we sing a prayer of both the "God of mercy," and of that "wild God." Auto-da-Fe could not abolish the Sabbath, nor could pogrom, nor gas chamber, nor bullet. As I write this it is still the Sabbath. And a week again there shall be another one. And the week after that, it shall come again. Forever, both here and in Squirrel Hill, and everywhere else where people are still capable of love.

The Jewish Woman in America, 2010

RACHEL MENNIES

I see them in Giant Eagle, buying the same soap and eggs as I buy; at the Squirrel Hill library,
their sons garbed as God prefers even in hot July, consoled by the tallit, trailing blessed white strings
through Forbes Avenue dirt. The women cover their heads, their skirts making dark mysteries
of their legs. All faith, they show me the fabric of inaccessible glory, the rents in my own life. My God holds
nobody responsible. He lives in the thick air over Philadelphia, likes it there, doesn't speak to me much, if at all. My God accepts
the muddle of our lives: reformed, distracted, desirous of strangers in other, wilder places. "As you wish," He says,
and retreats into the sunset alone. From Him, I wrest a path without limits, two strong and willful legs to bare to a street full of eyes.

Echo and Narcissus

RACHEL MENNIES

Narcissist, she sees omens everywhere.

It makes it possible for her to believe in God,

in her marriage, rippling beside her in the Mon.

She counts each cardinal in the trees, each green light

stacked one after the other on Fifth Avenue.

The world wrapped around her like a thicket, like a cave.

But the gods built the cardinals, each tree, each

of these three rivers. And some nights, while

her husband sleeps, she hears

the echo, pulsing through the East End like a siren

only her God-made ears can hear.

Lean over me, one bank at a time, and see

how you can make this last forever.

Now lean farther.
Lean farther.

November 18, 2016

RACHEL MENNIES

Naomi, the delicatessen on Murray keeps a placard in its window for the
Hasids.

It tracks the date of every Sabbath sundown, creeping earlier by the week.

(Our god lives closest to us in the dark, when the body and the spirit
cease distinction.)

Why do I always forget that the weather's different where you sleep?

I imagine you also cold, warming your body with your hands.

Beside me the other Jewish women, the visibly devout, queue for their
Shabbat ingredients.

Here the pink cow's tongue uncurls irresistibly, already smoked.

Here the animal haunches are stacked salted and glistening.

I long for you even here, standing before deli glass on a November
afternoon.

What if it's my desire that lengthens the night?

How the letters I write you cool once they leave my hands.

How the world holds itself so still in the frost, waiting.

PART 3

DOWNTOWN, NORTH, AND SOUTH

Downtown

RICH GEGICK

I've worked in Downtown restaurants for well over a decade. The neighborhood, more aptly described as a corridor, has transformed dramatically over the past thirteen years from a place where suburbanites were told to avoid after dark to a burgeoning nightlife spot packed with cocktail bars and chef-inspired restaurants with al fresco tables. Colorful umbrellas the color of those candy pills stuck to wax paper dot the sidewalks, and the trendy establishments on Sixth and Seventh Avenues as well as Market Square are packed full on Friday and Saturday nights.

When I first started as a busboy, the remnants of the red-light district remained. The old porno theaters had yet to be refurbished, and a few stalwart prostitutes sold their wares on Liberty Avenue between Ninth and Tenth Streets. Market Square was nothing more than a giant bus stop/open narcotics bazaar, a place management told me to avoid at night while dressed in my work uniform. Management instructed me on my first night to wear only my street clothes to and from work.

After dark, we service industry workers owned the streets. Like the river rats who dragged their greasy black tails from dumpster to dumpster, we roamed from bar to bar post-work. Places like Cigar Bar, 1902 Tavern, 245 Tavern, Doubleday's. These establishments were smoke filled dives that catered to us, the people who worked the then scant eateries of Downtown. In those places we were free to drink well tequila, pump the jukebox full of dollar bills, chase blistering affairs that burned out after a few nights or in the Sodom and Gomorrah, anything goes downstairs bathroom of the Cigar Bar. Free to slide dollar bills into the g-strings of the strip club dancers, as the only place open Sunday nights was Blush. Drinks on the house, heavy pours, empty streets, sex workers all gave Downtown a seedy, early Tom Waits vibe that as a 23-year-old writer searching for any kind of a voice (who also had a hard-on for Bukowski), I fell in love.

Nostalgia is a powerful dope for any native Pittsburgher, and I am prone to chase its high. Sunday morning polka radio, Steelers games on late fall afternoons with a pot of kielbasa and sauerkraut simmering on the stove. The places and things that aren't there anymore. The steel mill where my father worked still belching smoke and fire. *There's no Winky's in Wilmerding. You can't keep an Iron man down. You gonna like it. We are fam-a-lee.*

On any given night in this city, in any of the remaining old man bars on a neighborhood street corner like a pile of dirty socks, I can walk in and turn the clock back to whatever time I want. All it takes is an old song on the jukebox, and in these moments, I can't tell whether I am glorifying someone else's past or living my own future. The magnetic pull of remembering Pittsburgh as it was is such because for many of us, the way things are in this city now is as confusing as ever.

In the neighborhoods, especially those on the east end, high rise apartment buildings continue to sprout like dandelions after a spring rain. Many of these buildings charge over 1,000 dollars per month for a one-bedroom unit. A great proliferation of trendy bars and restaurants fill in the old storefronts. Rents and property values skyrocket and long-time tenants are forced to move. Zoning violations that were never enforced suddenly are, and home and business owners are charged heavy fines, sometimes forced to pack up and leave.

Gentrification is a buzzword, it's a dirty word. Over the past decade or so, money has poured into Pittsburgh and cities like it all across America. To us natives, this changing landscape produces a vertigo like feeling. We're dizzy, unable to tell whether our very identity is disappearing before our eyes, as we have invested so much of ourselves into our "place" in this country and the world. For many of us who were born in and around Pittsburgh, we can trace our American story back about 100 years to the very town, neighborhood, house, tenement where it began.

The people who move into these apartment buildings, who rent the places I used to rent at double the monthly cost, who stroll into the old bars as if they own the places, feel like invading hoards. A few years ago after work, I found myself in a punk bar up on Polish Hill with my then girlfriend. Among the graffiti in the men's room was a sticker that read, *Keep Pittsburgh Shitty.* There are similar guerilla marketing campaigns in cities across America, like *Keep Austin Weird*, or my favorite, *Youngstown Hates You.* All arise from this same sentiment of feeling invaded, of outsiders versus insiders. Real Pittsburgh versus fake, Whole Foods loving Pittsburgh.

A few years after I started working in town, the stuffily named "Cultural District" blossomed. Heinz Hall, The Benedum Center, the O'Reilly, all started running shows weekly including national music acts, touring productions of famous Broadway shows, comedians. Suddenly after dark on weekend nights, the streets were overrun with well-dressed people searching for post-show cocktails and appetizers. The demand was supplied. A local diner chain opened a two-floor restaurant with rooftop seating, featuring a chef intensive menu with locally sourced ingredients and craft spirits. Then another steakhouse opened. Then another. A local chef opened his take on a modern steakhouse right in the center of the theater district, then an overflow restaurant a few blocks away with a similar menu. Then a few years later the Japanese/Mexican fusion taco restaurant on the same block. Once the city decided to level and re-rout the busses away from Market Square, the downtown reclamation process really took off.

Through all the days where it seemed as though a new restaurant opened every week, downtown faced little gentrification strife. While the city has looked to attract people to rent apartments there in recent years, the actual living population has been relatively small for decades. Unlike Bloomfield, East Liberty, and Lawrenceville, there are few people who have been forced or left out as the money poured in from the Heinz Endowment and other city fathers to refurbish and rebuild it. A few businesses, restaurants, went belly up in the shifting landscape, and that's always a shame. I believe that those casualties, sad as they are, were the cost of doing business.

I can't say this great boom hasn't negatively affected my wallet. There are simply more options available. In the decrepit downtown, my restaurant was the only game in town for any number of the events taking place. Now, our white tablecloth, classic steakhouse food, service, and atmosphere is reserved mostly for special occasions like birthdays, graduations, and wedding anniversaries. On game nights, concert nights, people desire something a bit more casual and more fun than a clubby, dark steakhouse. I can't blame them.

Now, when I leave work on a spring and summer weekend night, the whole corridor is alive. People going to and from shows, taking the walk back across the Clemente Bridge from the Pirates game. In Market Square, ragtime jazz oozes from the New Orleans style restaurant and sticks to the humid air. The valets are busy well into the late night parking BMWs and Mercedes. Suburban people dressed in collared shirts and sundresses long warned to avoid Downtown like the plague make the trek to dine, dance, and carry on.

It's easy to say downtown was better before all this. Nostalgia is a protective posture designed to shield my identity in a city and in a greater world that has undergone rapid and sometimes frightening change. What does it mean to be a Pittsburgher? I can't say I have an answer anymore. The old landmarks fade, the old ways of life die when the older generations pass on, replaced with new landmarks, new ways of life that are not better or worse, just different. What am I mourning when I complain about how Downtown was better a decade ago? What's to miss about crime, drugs, and prostitution? And who, exactly, was displaced in this revival?

I'm mourning nothing. So come Downtown. It's a nice place. Just save a stool for me and my co-workers on Saturday night.

Can a Sports-Crazed City Turn a Theater Person into a Baseball Person?

SHANNON REED

Shannon Reed thought she knew what kind of fan she was, until she moved back home to Pittsburgh.

All Pittsburghers, even those who can't be bothered with baseball, know what happened on October 13, 1960: the Pirates' second baseman, Bill Mazeroski, hit a walk-off home run, which shot over the left field fence of Forbes Field in Oakland, and into history, securing for the Pirates the World Series in the seventh game. In the photos of Mazeroski rounding third and heading for home, the joy is palpable, as teammates and fans rush toward him, arms extended, faces actually aglow. Forbes Field, where the game was played, arches upward in the background, almost like a sanctuary; apt, because that home run was miraculous. The city exploded with happiness.

I was born 14 years too late to witness it, but grew up in a Pirates-loving household two hours east of Pittsburgh. People in Johnstown still talked about Mazeroski's miracle in the late 1980s. My dad went to a banquet then at the Holiday Inn downtown at which Mazeroski received an award. Dad took to recapping his conversation with the slugger as often as possible in the weeks following it, and people always listened intently, as though some great wisdom were being passed along, instead of a simple exchange of pleasantries.

But I rolled my eyes every time he told the story. Back then, I thought Mazeroski's triumph was ancient history, something vaguely important, but that had happened a long time ago on a field far, far away. I was busy defining myself as a theater kid, so Pittsburgh's allure was in the promise of high school drama club trips to see touring Broadway shows at the Benedum Center downtown. I liked baseball well enough, more than any other sport, having played catcher on a Little League team for a few years. But still, I wasn't especially keen on it, even when the Pirates made it to the postseason in 1990, 1991, and 1992.

Even though great baseball was still happening in Pittsburgh, it seemed to me at 16, 17, and 18 that the best days of the sport in the city were far behind. This, I know now, is what history does. It telescopes, so that dozens of years compress into one memory, while the present moves serenely forward at its usual stately pace. The thousands of past years you did not experience blend together, while those in your own recent past are distinct as memory. Thus, I saw the Pirates' days of triumph, long before I was born, as history, while my then-present awareness of the team, with their parade of good and bad games, fair and foul seasons, were memories that couldn't compete with past glories frozen, triumphant, in time.

But when I enrolled in the MFA program at the University of Pittsburgh in 2012, suddenly the history of Pirates baseball became real to me. Walking around the campus one day I stumbled upon the actual physical remnants of those glory days. From 1909 to the 1970 season, the Pittsburgh Pirates had played on Forbes Field, and now its back wall, flag pole, and home base are preserved on Pitt's campus, an athletic shrine in the heart of an academic neighborhood. The carefully preserved fragments immediately reminded me of the abandoned, disintegrating cathedrals, abbeys, and chapels I had visited in Ireland. Great wonders had been glimpsed here, seen by the community, but now all was quiet.

––––––––––––

Forbes Field must have been something else, once upon a time. Barney Dreyfuss, the Pirates' team owner in the early 1900s, purchased the land for it, adjacent to the iconic Pittsburgh sites of Schenley Park and the main branch of the Carnegie Library, with financial help from Andrew Carnegie himself. Designed by Charles Wellford Leavitt, Jr., the stadium Dreyfuss paid for was three tiers of concrete and steel. It was the first of its kind at a time when wooden stadiums dotted the nation, and entrepreneurs were still trying to figure out how to make money off of baseball. Its innovations included a sort of green room for the umpires, a clubhouse for the visiting teams, and ramps to help move spectators more easily through the stadium. The steel framework was painted light green, the roof red, and the beige terracotta designs spelled out signage reading "Pennsylvania Athletic Club." On opening day, over 30,000 people packed into the stadium, and the announcers, overwhelmed by the vast immensity of the field, had troubled estimating how far hit balls had traveled. After the game, a weeping Dreyfuss told assembled reporters that it was the happiest day of his life.

Now, though, it's a ghost field, a lost cathedral. I learned that the University of Pittsburgh bought the land from the Pirates in 1958, agreeing to allow the Bucs to use it until they had a new place to play. In 1970, the Pirates—and the Steelers, who had also occasionally used the field—moved to the brand-new Three Rivers Stadium on the North Shore of the city. And in 1971, Pitt tore down Forbes Field. Giant, Brutalist-style university buildings were built where it had been, with Forbes Field's home plate tucked into the ground floor of one of them as a shrine, allowing those with very good imaginations—or actual memories of what had been—to stand in the middle of a soaring academic foyer and imagine Bill Mazeroski stepping up to the plate on a fateful day in 1960. I found that I could stand inside at the plate, students buzzing by, and imagine a pitch and a swing, then the crack of the hit ball, before making my way through the foyer, out a double set of doors, across a busy intersection, to a piece of the left-field wall, where I turned to imagine that ball flying toward me.

There are places on this planet, I believe, where the ground has been hallowed. It's absorbed some specific feeling—trauma, joy, change—and radiates it back to those visiting, even hundreds of years later. I'm not alone in this belief; it's why people visit Pearl Harbor; the Church of the Nativity in Jerusalem; those bombed or abandoned cathedrals across the ocean; and, less majestically, the home plate and left-field wall that used to be part of Forbes Field. The only way to absorb a certain kind of understanding is to stand in the spot where history happened.

Forbes Field is gone, but its steadfast companions remain. Schenley Park drifts greenly away from campus, while the Carnegie Library is a bustling destination for every age. And Pitt's Cathedral of Learning remains, too. Standing 42 stories in its distinctive Late Gothic Revival style, it's visible from miles around, thanks to a location on a vast lawn that is surrounded by much shorter buildings. Pitt Chancellor John G. Bowman came up with the idea for it in 1921, writing of a "tower singing upward that would tell the story of Pittsburgh." The eventual building was dedicated in 1937, with a mandate both much narrower and much broader. The idea of telling the story of Pittsburgh is long gone, and instead the Cathedral's mission ends up being less about the city's history and more about being an actual cathedral: a gathering place for the community, where the sacred and common intertwine.

The Cathedral used to be adjacent to Forbes Field and now stands as the centerpiece to Pitt's sprawling campus. A handful of older people I've met remember gathering on the Cathedral's high-up balconies to watch the

Bucs battle their rivals on the field far below.

When I arrived at Pitt, I knew as little about the Cathedral as I did about the Bucs. I was still a theater person, with that same vague response to baseball, neither especially interested nor bored. Coincidentally, I had left Western Pennsylvania for college in Ohio in 1992, the last year the Pirates would be playoff contenders for two decades. All I heard about them from then on were complaints from my father and brother, which seemed even more distant after I moved to New York to get a graduate degree at NYU, and ended up staying for years. As I went about my life in Brooklyn, the Pirates might as well have been preserved in amber, along with bobby sox and poodle skirts, or stonewashed jeans and spiral perms.

In New York, you had to be one thing. You could be into opera, or Colonial history, or exotic birds, or a million other things, but you had to specialize. The offerings of the city are so dense and comprehensive, and the city so demanding with its crowds, subways, and sheer size, that there's no time to be more than one kind of person. I fully committed to being a Theater Person (the grown-up version of that theater kid). I ran from the experimental theaters in SoHo to Broadway, and made my living writing plays and teaching theater. There was almost no time left to take in any sports for the 14 years I lived there. The staff at the theater publishing company I briefly worked at went to see the Mets once, and I remember feeling surprisingly at home and content as I watched the rituals of the game unfold. But I very rarely went back.

In 2012, when I flew to Pittsburgh to interview at Pitt before joining their MFA program, it was easy to ignore sports for the 36 hours I was there. I took in a show at City Theatre, the city's celebrated incubator of new works, and interviewed with another theater company. "It'll be easy to be a Theater Person here," I thought. I vaguely noticed that almost everyone I passed, even at the theaters or on campus, was wearing something black and gold, the colors of the Steelers, Bucs, and Penguins, but this didn't concern me. Instead, I stood at the edge of the Commons Room on the first floor of the Cathedral, peering up at the vaulted ceilings and across the half-acre space at dozens of students intently reading. Here, I knew, books, writing, education, and the arts were valued. When Pitt offered me the position, I said yes.

After I decided to move, my brother, who had also gone to Pitt for a graduate degree, warned me that sports were a *thing* in the 'Burgh. I nodded: sure, I knew that. In what big city were sports not a thing? We had Baseball People in New York of two varieties, three if you counted the Brooklyn Cyclones, a minor league team. It would be fine. There were Theater People in Pittsburgh, as well. To each their own.

I hadn't discovered the back wall of Forbes Field yet, hadn't stumbled upon the photograph of the Cathedral and the baseball stadium yet, didn't yet know that a walk through any array of office cubicles at Pitt would reveal Terrible Towels (a hallowed Steeler fan tradition) draped behind countless desks, hadn't noticed that something like 80 percent of the cars here have a team logo on them. I hadn't marked an October 13 by quietly walking around the faithful observers reliving the Mazeroski home run where the ballpark used to be. I didn't grasp what sports meant to Pittsburgh yet. I didn't really understand what my brother was trying to tell me.

It wasn't until I moved here that I began to see. Of course, at first, everything around me was new: people, commutes, books, tasks. But slowly, I began to experience the city. When I took public transportation to a show at the Symphony, the sign on the bus's front reminded me to cheer, "Here We Go, Steelers!" Next to me at the concert, a man sat attentively listening to a violin solo, his Penguins jersey neatly pressed. Grad student friends who worked three jobs somehow found the means to pay for cable so that they could watch the games. My church cut short an event so we could get home in time for the opening kickoff. In the schools where I presented workshops, from Hazelwood to Washington, rows of children sat in black and gold.

I was charmed, but confused until I understood what my brother had been trying to tell me. People joke that "Pittsburghese," with its "yinz" and "farwood" and "sammichs," is the local dialect, but actually, it's sports. And if I wanted to live here, I needed to learn to speak it. But I don't really care about football, and actively dislike hockey, so I resisted. I was a Theater Person. Theater! That was my jam!

And then, the Pirates got good again.

PNC Park, the Pirates current home, is the first they don't have to share with any other sports team in the city. Sure, they rent it out for an occasional event or concert, but the ballpark is theirs alone, with the Steelers' Heinz Field just a stone's throw away on the North Shore, which lies across the Allegheny River from downtown Pittsburgh. Downtown is hemmed in by those famous three rivers—the Ohio, the Allegheny, and the Monongahela; placing PNC on the North Shore was justified as a way of boosting businesses in that area, a proposition that seems less true the further from the stadium one travels. The stadium has proven to be a mixed bag for city residents. It serves as a cathedral, of course, and one that I find astoundingly accessible when compared to the epic trek to any New York City stadium. But it has also increased traffic, congestion, and the number of drunken fans in a previously quieter section of the city. And sometimes it seems to serve only members of its congregation instead of being a cathedral for all.

Yet, despite a distinctly terrible name, PNC is beloved among baseball's congregants, and is widely considered to be one of the best stadiums in the country. Opened in 2001, it was designed to harken back to classic ballparks, perhaps as a rebuke to Three Rivers Stadium, about which, the best most fans could say was that it was "functional." From many seats at PNC, you look out across the ball field to the river, crossed by the Roberto Clemente, Andy Warhol, and David McCullough Bridges, and then to the beautiful downtown Pittsburgh skyline.

On a visit home from Brooklyn, I made my first visit to PNC with my dad and brother. I was much more enthralled by the view than by the game. As the sun set, the buildings glowed, golden and pink, and I barely noticed that the Pirates were behind by 10 points in the seventh inning. I was 28, and it was a beautiful night in a big city, and I almost didn't care that I could barely follow what my father and brother were talking about—batting averages, maybe? It didn't matter. I was content to be there.

I spent the fall of 2012 and winter of 2013 settling into my new home in Pittsburgh. I made it to a performance in nearly every theater and branched out to the symphony, local art galleries, and a dance concert. I went for hikes in the nearby state parks, and saw the architectural marvel that is Frank Lloyd Wright's Fallingwater. I visited coffee houses and restaurants. And it seemed as if I kept meeting the same people over and over, running into friends I knew from the MFA program at the opera, and spotting artist acquaintances at a nearby state park. I was beginning to see that Pittsburgh was a place where you could be more than one kind of person. When I heard the buzz that the Pirates were looking good for once, I was interested, remembering the happiness I'd felt at baseball games in the past. I knew I could surely use that feeling of contentment again, in my busy, stressful life. But I was scared of the way sports seemed to encompass some fans in Pittsburgh. Could I just dip my toe into baseball fandom? Could I learn to speak the real Pittsburghese?

Of course, the answer is yes. My father and brother swept into town one Spring evening in 2013 and I joined them in what one does if one is a Reed and going to a baseball game in the 'Burgh: you load up on meats and carbs at Max's Allegheny Tavern, a long-running German restaurant on the North Shore, and then you park close to The Pittsburgh Fan, a sports merchandise store on Federal Street, across from PNC, where you buy a new T-shirt or hat. After that stop, it's a straight shot past the Roberto Clemente statue and into the ballpark, where every seat is pretty good.

Even after a mere six months back in the 'Burgh, I had already developed a defensiveness about the city, the result of too many well-meaning New York friends telling me, consolingly, "I hear it's really *very* nice there, now that the steel mills have closed." But even I was surprised at how pleasant it all was: the warm spring night, the diversity of the crowd, an interesting game shaping up in front of me, my dad and brother already chowing down on hot dogs, even though we'd just eaten. Pittsburgh, looming familiarly, spread out across from us. I could see the roof of the theater I'd been at a few nights before, and knew that the decorative brick facade of Heinz Hall was hiding just out of sight. There was a buzzing sound from the boats on the river. Next to me, a man explained to his grandson that they would have to stand soon for the national anthem. I looked over the field, and felt a strange sense of relief: no play was going to be performed, and I did not need to have an opinion about the set, direction, or players. I could just watch, lazily, not a Theater Person, and certainly not a Baseball Person, but just…a Pittsburgher, it seemed, someone who could appreciate the skill of anything, without being a maniac about it. This felt lovely.

The Pirates won. And when I went back a few weeks later, this time with a friend, they won again. As it turns out, they started to win a lot, and I liked it. Real fans of a team love them whether they win or lose, I know, but I wasn't yet a real fan, I guess. I liked it when we won. I still do. I like to be in a crowd that leaps to its feet cheering. I like it when the players run off the field happy, pointing out and up at us, as if we helped somehow, the cathedral of baseball lit up around them, neon green in the darkness. Good baseball wasn't ancient history in Pittsburgh anymore; it was happening, now. Lots of things were happening in Pittsburgh now, actually, and some of them were very good, indeed.

I started going to games more regularly, then leaving them on the television in the background at home once in a while, then making sure I'd be home to grade papers so I could watch. I lined up dates to go to PNC. I grew my collection of gold and black clothing. I became a person who knew a few stats—such as that 2013 was the Pirates' first winning season since 1992—and then a person who knew all of the players' names, and then someone who could tweet reasonable opinions on the players, of the sort that merited a reply from a *Pittsburgh Tribune-Review* sports writer. Last Christmas, my brother gave me a Pirates baseball hat, the first I'd owned since I played Little League, 30 years before. I still feel as if I'm pretending when I wear it, but you know what? No one ever calls me on it.

Pittsburgh has many problems. It grieves me especially that some of my African-American students do not feel the same freedoms that I do, nor assume their opportunities extend beyond fields of play. I think often of Forbes Field, and the Cathedral of Learning, and PNC Park, never forgetting that full integration has only been a given at the last of them. History telescopes, but some memories linger far past the lifespans of those who made them.

But I find hope in one thing that the city does well, and that is to provide cathedrals for us to gather. We show up a community, and, together, we go about our business of worshipping, thinking, sitting, reading, watching, whatever it is we feel called upon to do. Eventually, by being together, we may grow into people of tolerance who understand that we're all fully human. None of us need to specialize—although we certainly can if we want to—but we can all be Theater People, or Baseball People, or whatever else catches our fancy, all at once. We are flawed, broken people. But we love our teams, and one of our teams is humanity.

I know this is true because of what happens on October 13th when, year after year, fans gather at the old flagpole to listen to a broadcast of Mazeroski's game. At the 2015 event, an announcer led the crowd in a moment of silence for Yogi Berra, who had died a few days before. In 1960, the Yankee catcher had watched Mazeroski's homer sail away, along with the Yankees' World Series dreams. Bowing their heads, modern-day Bucs fans saluted him as an icon whose sojourn in the ordinariness of the present had finally come to an end. He was now consigned to history, to be winnowed into a few stories and moments. Then the announcer said, "They say you can't turn back the clock. Nonsense. We will." As the audience stood among the bits and pieces of the old field, listening with anticipation to a re-broadcast of the entire game, they did.

Let history telescope us, as it will, a fact I am all too aware of this season, for my father has attended his last Bucs game, slipping out of this life just a day after watching the team sail towards their third post-season in a row in 2015. This season, our second without him, as my brother and I went back to Max's, then The Pittsburgh Fan, then the game, we missed our dad. I always miss him. My mother comes along to the games sometimes now, because she, too, has grown to love the Bucs, even in a not-great season like this one, and she, too, misses the guy who first brought us all to PNC. We will stay Baseball People at least partly because Dad was, too, and this will connect us, even as history continues to telescope him further and further away from us.

But while I am sometimes sad at PNC Park and sometimes miss those days of easier fandom when I was on my feet and cheering a win more often than not, I also feel that familiar contentment that comes from watching a game unfold. Because in Pittsburgh, despite our pride in a past both glorious and difficult, as well as in the cathedrals we built back then, we know we can only live in the present. And even though a mediocre season is just ending, it won't be long before the boys of summer will be back on the North Side, getting ready for batting practice to begin.

Exile Poems

TUHIN DAS

Translated from the Bengali by Arunava Sinha

1.
There's a country within each of us.
Neighbors walk their dogs in the park.
In the morning I wait for bus No. 54
on Arch Street, I work at a call center.
When I talk to people in distant lands,
my country is always within me. Some ask:
"Where are you from? Do you miss your home?"
I have borne my country from afar, I tell them:
"Do you know how light a country is, like the feathers
of your robins." The wind blows south from the north,
and I remember the Bay of Bengal.
There's a country within each of us.

2.
The bus moves along the 16th Street Bridge,
I stare at the distant hills where I'm going on work,
it's raining outside—I find myself resembling Zen poets
in some way, so I take Ikkyū's poems from my bag to read.

3.
The houses on Sampsoina Way are silent. I have
dissolved the black night in red wine. I go for walks
very early in the morning. At the end of the night shift
at Allegheny General Hospital I often see you
in your nurse's uniform walking along the road
that runs through the park.

Notes: Numbered according to the poems
1. Arch Street is a street in Northside, Pittsburgh, Pennsylvania.
The Bay of Bengal is located in the north-eastern part of the Indian Ocean.
Bangladesh, the country of my birth, is situated to its north.

2. "The David McCullough Bridge, commonly and historically known as the 16ᵗʰ Street Bridge, is a steel trussed through arch bridge that spans the Allegheny River in Pittsburgh, Pennsylvania."
Ikkyū Sōjun (1394-1481) was a Japanese Buddhist monk and Zen poet. I often read his volume of poems titled 'Crow with No Mouth', edited by Stephen Berg, published by Copper Canyon Press.

3. "Sampsonia Way is not your typical Pittsburgh alley. Over the years, Mattress Factory art projects and City of Asylum have transformed the outsides of several houses along Sampsonia, adding another surreal layer to the intrigue."—Patricia Lowry, "Google makes the world a stage for Sampsonia Way", *Pittsburgh Post-Gazette*, November 12, 2008
"Allegheny General Hospital is a large urban hospital located at 320 East North Avenue in Pittsburgh, Pennsylvania."

They Just Used Them to Go Everywhere

SHERRIE FLICK

For Edward Waldo (1935-2018)

I bribe my across-the-street neighbor, Ed Waldo, with a homemade pop-pyseed cake and he agrees to come over and talk to me with my recorder on. He's 80 years old, ornery and unsteady on his feet, so my husband Rick escorts him up the stairs from his house to the boardwalk and across Holt Street to our place on the South Side Slopes. Because Waldo's home is on the river side of the street below the massive retaining wall, just to get from his door to the curb requires walking up a small flight of city steps. Once in the front door, a dog treat for my Yorkie, Bubby, magically appears in his hand. Bubby is a big Waldo fan. In good weather, Waldo (as he's always been known) sits outside his house with a variety of dog treats for all of the Slopes dogs that pass on their daily walks.

Waldo was born and raised in the house he now lives in, a bright pink, three-story home easily spotted from the Birmingham Bridge. He left for stints in Beechview and a raucous-sounding move to Florida, but after his mother died in 1990 he moved back. He strongly believes the spirits of both his mother and grandmother reside there with him.

He's a constant and natural storyteller equipped with a seemingly photographic memory. As we get him settled into a comfy chair, he's ready to talk stairs. He also talks sausages, newspaper routes, killing chickens (and pigeons), driving a chicken delivery truck, dance halls, the mill, vintage cars and the Steelers.

Today, we focus on the crazy city staircases that surround us. Growing up, everyone in his family walked the steps. His mom, his dad, everyone in the neighborhood. "You'd have to," he says, gesturing widely with his big hands. "They just used them to go everywhere. On Saturdays, my mom would say, 'Let's go,' and we'd grab the empty shopping bags and we'd start going down and shop, and both of us would be carrying the shopping bags up."

It was a walking community back then. Waldo can't remember seeing more than four or five cars on our street, which is now packed nose-to-nose with them. Not only did everyone know each other, they were also—I come to realize—pretty much related in one way or another. Most everyone—at least on our end of the Slopes—was Polish. "When I was a kid nobody spoke English up here," Waldo says. "It was broken English. And the neighbors would talk to each other in Polish. ... They used to call it Hunky Hill because everybody worked in the mill."

People walked the steps, zipping up and down to work, to visit friends, neighbors, or the many small local businesses (now defunct) that lined the streets—candy stores, corner stores, bars, dance halls, a tailor—were just a staircase or two up, down or over. There were as many small businesses up as down back then, which in my mind immediately gives the city steps of the past more purpose.

Waldo can still recite the stair routes he took to deliver his newspapers, from Holt Street up to Arlington. To him, this entire place is still very much alive with ghosts from his past. The place itself seems to be a member of Waldo's family. When I ask him what he loves about living on the Slopes, he says with a laugh, "I'm stuck with it."

It seems that I'm stuck with it too. In walking the city steps of my neighborhood, I've come to understand its history in a deeper, more exacting way. And in living on the Slopes we've become part of its history, too.

I remember a crazy winter morning in February 2010 when the snow had packed-in the entire city overnight. They called it Snowmageddon, and our street was plowed in, not out, for two weeks. That morning unveiled thigh-high snow drifts. Not one car could enter or leave our neighborhood. Rick and I strapped on our hiking packs and walked door to door through the crisp air, a bright blue sky for a backdrop. We took orders for bread, prescriptions, beer and whiskey for our elderly neighbors. Waldo wanted white bread and I insisted we buy him wheat, which didn't go over well once we got back to his house. We hiked down to the Giant Eagle and stocked up, and then we walked back up the difficult staircases, delivering packages door to door. That Snowmageddon city step hike fit us into part of the larger Slopes' story on our little street, part of Waldo's repertoire, connecting us to generations who walked the stairs in the past and those who will come huffing up them in the future.

The Bars of Dormont

VINCE GUERRIERI

We started at the top of the hill, where Mount Lebanon turns into Dormont as Washington Road turns into West Liberty Avenue, at Cain's, and must have hit just about every bar on the way down West Liberty, ending at the Apple Inn. It had been that kind of day.

I was 22, less than a year out of college, and had covered my first multi-county killing spree. The day started out innocuously enough. I was out in Oakdale, interviewing the 99-year mayor, which was the hardest news I expected to cover that day. It was Friday. It was payday.

As I was wrapping up the interview, I got a call from my boss at the late, lamented South Hills bureau for the Pittsburgh Trib. *Synagogue. Shots fired. Hate crime. Coroner. County homicide.* Slowly we realized that all the reports were related.

Richard Baumhammers grew up in Mt. Lebanon in a solid upper middle-class family. He was a lawyer, admitted to the bar in Georgia and Pennsylvania. He was also profoundly mentally ill.

That day, the Reds were in town to play the Pirates, and I was thinking of going to the baseball game. That day he woke up, went to his Jewish next-door neighbor's house and shot her. He then drove down to her synagogue and popped off a couple shots there before going off to his next target.

Baumhammers went to Scott Town Center and opened fire in an Indian grocery store next to the Subway we'd go to on Tuesdays for $4 footlongs. He killed one man instantly. The other was paralyzed, dying seven years later. He probably drove past my apartment in Carnegie, and then shot at another synagogue before hopping on the Parkway West outbound.

I got to Robinson Town Centre shortly after he departed, leaving a trail of carnage in his wake. The police hadn't even taped off the Japanese restaurant where he'd walked in, pulled a .357 Magnum out of his briefcase and fatally shot two men. I watched them take the bodies out as a freshly minted widow wailed.

It was a beautiful day, and the combination of a bright blue sky, massive trauma and a newsroom springing en masse into action turned out to be a dress rehearsal for less than 18 months later, when buildings toppled in New York City and reports of a hijacked plane over Pittsburgh led us to believe we'd be next. The ill feelings of the Baumhammers shootings washed over me again nearly two decades later when I heard initial reports about another xenophobe in Allegheny County going on a killing spree involving a synagogue, and my blood ran cold.

I drove past the ballgame traffic at Three Rivers Stadium to the Trib newsroom on the third floor of the D.L. Clark Building on the North Shore. It wasn't often I made it to the main newsroom, and every trip still felt aspirational to me. There was always a tension between the main newsroom and the three suburban bureaus. Editors on the suburban desk blew smoke up our asses, saying we were just as important as the reporters in the main newsroom. Editors in the main newsroom used exile to the bureaus as a threat.

Less than two months before Baumhammers' spree, a black man, Ronald Taylor, decided to kill as many white people as he could in Wilkinsburg. It wasn't far from our Monroeville bureau, but the bylines in the next day's paper were almost exclusively reporters from the main newsroom. "If something like that happened here, would they do the same thing to us," I asked our bureau chief. The question was a stunning mix of bravado and insecurity, and could only be asked by a reporter fresh out of j-school who felt he had something to prove. She couldn't answer it. As it turns out, I got the answer I wanted. But it wasn't what I wanted.

What I wanted after that harrowing day was a drink. As luck would have it, I had a co-worker that did as well.

There were three other people in the bureau's newsroom. Two were middle-aged married women with children to go home to. The other was Paul. He was a decade older than I was, and grew up in Peters Township, a rapidly suburbanizing community just over the county line into Washington County. His journalism career had taken him to Maryland and then back to the Pittsburgh area, and was more than willing to go out for a drink once in a while. He could be an angry drunk, but given the circumstances in his life at that point, I can't necessarily blame him (and as someone who's let more people than I care to admit see me at my worst, I can't cast aspersions). I heard him talk occasionally about a woman who got away. He was living with his mother after his parents divorced but his heart—and his liver—belonged to Dormont.

We started at the Dormont/Mt. Lebanon line at Cain's. Paul wasn't a tremendous fan of Cain's. He felt like it was a Dormont bar that was pretentious because it wanted to be a Mount Lebanon bar. In a way, he was probably right. John Cain, the bar's owner and namesake, had some involvement in the Mt. Lebanon Saloon and the Ugly Dog in Green Tree, and all three had a similar feel.

It was your standard neighborhood bar, with dark wood, reasonably cheap beer (if you drank what was on special that night) and enough windows that it didn't move the needle on the dive scale of the night sports editor at the Trib, who said the diveyness of a bar is in inverse proportion to the number of windows it has. It was the kind of place that you could shoot a cannon through and not hit anyone at 9 p.m. But two hours later, it was packed to the gills, with most of the patrons wearing white dress shirts and black pants. After the nice restaurants nearby closed and the staff wanted to go somewhere for a drink to unwind, they ended up at Cain's—a ringing endorsement to me.

We walked down West Liberty Avenue, skipping past the Suburban Room. Its 1950s-chic sign and façade suggested the kind of place you'd see the Rat Pack chaining Luckies—or a film noir detective kicking back a martini, waiting for the femme fatale to vamp into his life. It wasn't the kind of place we were looking for that particular night.

Our next stop was Sam's. It scored a little higher on the diveyness scale, and it was Paul's favorite watering hole. It put on no airs—and in fact was the place where I learned of that Pittsburgh tradition of leaving your money on the bar.

I spent six years in Pittsburgh, and I sometimes felt like some kind of anthropologist there, being exposed to a culture alien from my own. One of those traits was a strange trusting nature—and a reciprocity of that trust. It's not uncommon to see folding chairs on the side of the street to hold a parking space—and other drivers respect the sanctity of the lawn chairs! It's also not uncommon in bars, particularly working class ones like Sam's, to see a stack of bills sitting next to someone's drink— sometimes with the money and drink unattended while the patron was tapping a kidney! Paul would point, the bartender would fill his glass or bring another bottle and take a couple bucks off the pile. "Aren't you worried someone will try and walk off with that," I asked. "Anyone who did that would get the shit beat out of them," he told me. He covered a lot of the same crime and calamity I did, but in that instance, his faith in his fellow human beings remained secure.

After Sam's, we walked across the street to Cip's. At one point, it was referred to as the Cheers of Dormont, the place where everyone knew everyone else, and the crowd included local luminaries like players for the Steelers and the Penguins. But by the time I came to the Pittsburgh area, the place was on its last legs. The ambience left a little to be desired, so we had our drink and left.

The next stop was Slap Shots, probably the most popular bar in Dormont—for good or for ill. It seemed like all the angry drunks in town ended up there, as evidenced in the police reports I had to read regularly. One threw a shot glass at a bartender and was escorted out by local law enforcement. Another tried to kick the back window out of the cruiser. (By comparison, the drunks in Crafton, another community I covered, were downright penitent. I remember reading a report of police finding a pickup truck halfway up a telephone pole. Police opened the door and had about eight empty beer cans spill out. The driver said, "You got me." What else could he do?)

It was a dark bar for a dark night of the soul. I'd like to tell you that evening that we bonded and gained a deeper understanding of the profession we'd chosen. I'd like to tell you we reveled in doing the Lord's work, comforting the afflicted. It's not true. We drank beer and smoked cigarettes after we came down from the exhilaration of covering the most serious type of breaking news there is.

Being a crime reporter is like the beginning of *Saving Private Ryan*, when the officer at the front of the landing craft yells, "Remember your training and you will survive!" You run on pure instinct and adrenaline, and the more you do it, the better you get at it. (Until I got into middle age and started to realize I had some skill as a writer, I legitimately thought being a cops reporter was the only thing I was good at.) It's once you come down that you start to realize and contemplate the enormity of what you saw and covered that day, and it leaves you staring into a drink, firing one cigarette of the next. And the real deal with the devil is that it ruins you for every other beat at the paper. Covering sports seems like frivolity. Government is boring. You understand the old saw in journalism that the profession will kill you, but it'll keep you alive right up until it does.

At this point, we kind of had a sense of what we were doing, so we figured we might as well make the full sweep. We walked past the Vasta Lounge—we'd come back at the end of our odyssey for hangover aversion therapy with a late-night dinner at Tom's Diner next door, and could still hear the thumping bass from the bar's DJ; it wasn't quite our scene—to the Apple. Dormont's a compact borough, just a mile square, and we'd covered a half-mile from Cain's down to the Apple Inn on West Liberty at Potomac

Avenue. It was what passed for an accomplishment on a day that started out so nice but turned out to be utterly bereft of joy.

I went out drinking with Paul a few more times. We sang karaoke once at Slap Shots (I sang Sinatra; he sang the Doors). He got a better job in Florida, and we had his going-away party at Sam's. By then, the bureau newsroom had swelled to eight people. We were starting to put out zoned editions and needed as many warm bodies as we could find.

There's a concept called the third place, that people need a spot outside of work and home. That was especially apparent for me at that point. At work, I was fed a steady diet of crime and calamity. Some of the harrowing details still stick with me. A guy who beat his wife so violently she miscarried was charged with criminal homicide against an unborn child. His wife wouldn't testify against him. A kid drinking underage and looking for a fight found one—and got fatally stabbed. A mailman fatally shot by what turned out to be a child playing with a gun. I lived alone in a city I'd moved to for a job—not because I had friends or family there. I needed someplace to go to decompress after a day at work that was traumatic one way or another.

In time, I became a regular at Cain's. My favorite episode of *The Twilight Zone* is probably "Walking Distance," where Gig Young goes back to his childhood hometown—and discovers it's his childhood. One of the overarching themes of the episode is that everyone gets one idyllic time and place. In the litany of watering holes I've had, mine was Cain's. The wood paneling was warm and welcoming, the wizened bartender called me "Hemingway," and the regulars filled my soul with cheer.

I even got a girl's number there once. I mean, she never called me back, but in a way, I was kind of glad. Women come and go, but a good watering hole is forever. Or so I thought.

Ultimately, the Trib closed down the South Hills Bureau, and most of us ended up in the main newsroom, where sadism appeared to be a management strategy, particularly since the bureau chief who'd polished my copy and honed my reporting skills found another job at the newspaper. I started looking for drinking spots closer to the North Side. Sometimes, I didn't even leave the building, drinking at the Clark Bar downstairs. (We tried to avoid it before Pirates games, though. Not only was it almost prohibitively crowded, an alert copy editor discovered their prices were higher on gameday.)

I still found time to get to Cain's, at one point bringing the girl I was dating—who would ultimately become my wife. Everyone at the bar turned around to say hi to me as I walked past. "Uh, I've been here twice," I told her. She didn't believe me, but knew I was the type of person who made friends easily.

At the Trib, I was punted over to the sports copy desk, where we'd put the paper to bed and then stop at the Park House on East Ohio Street. For the Pittsburgh media, it was like Rick's in "Casablanca." You'd see guys there from the Trib, the Post-Gazette and Channel 11. Mike Lange from the Penguins would drink there—and put up with more of our drunken antics than we had any reason to expect him to.

In the end, I left Pittsburgh (but I still carry the accent with me). My going-away party was at Cain's. From what I remember, it was a really good time. That stretch of West Liberty Avenue changed. The restaurant across the street from Cain's, which went through several name changes when I was there, was razed. The Suburban Room became Jamison's, its sleek exterior now papered over with beer posters. Cip's closed in 2003, reopened in 2012 and closed again. Tom's Diner is gone.

Even Cain's is different now, and I'm not sure what to make of it. It's gone upscale.

A Miracle in Beltzhoover

BRITTANY HAILER

Paul Lee and his younger brother Andy say they witnessed a miracle when they were boys. Now middle-aged, they recall this memory with fondness and fascination. Their belief in it hasn't wavered.

They were boys, Paul 8 and Andy 7. Their mother had given them both new bikes for Christmas. They rushed out of the house. At the top of the hill, Paul went first. Andy followed closely behind. They careened, wind whooshing by their ears, hearts racing. The road made a sharp turn at the bottom of the hill. They knew it would. They'd done this a hundred times.

What they never saw before were two cars. Right in front of them.

Andy was behind Paul and in the fast-slow way accidents happen, he knew his brother was going to smash into the cars. He knew he would soon follow.

But then something unexpected happened. Andy said a man appeared and moved Paul to safety, right between the two cars. The man also guided Andy through the vehicles. Neither driver noticed. The man, angel, ghost, whatever he was, disappeared. Paul and Andy, panting, stared at each other. What had just happened? They were shaking.

Paul grabbed Andy's shoulder and said to him, "Andy, remember what just happened today. Don't ever forget it."

Years later, when Andy and Paul were 19 and 20, they devised a plan to start selling cocaine from New York in Pittsburgh. Andy said they thought their endeavor would be like the movie "Scarface." Paul had recently dropped out of the New York Institute of Technology and came back to Pittsburgh. The University of Pittsburgh had just kicked Andy out of school. The brothers were young, forced to start over.

Two years later, both brothers had become addicted. Andy burned out quickly and got clean, but Paul continued to use for almost two decades.

Their drug enterprise entangled some of their siblings. When Andy, now 51, admitted this at his kitchen table in Sheraden a month ago, he broke down and cried. He and Paul introduced their family to drugs, and it has had disastrous effects.

Years earlier, when Paul was at the height of his drug addiction and barely surviving, Andy asked him if he remembered the miracle.

"There's a reason that we went through that together," Andy remembered saying to Paul. "We're going to have to come out of this drug addiction together, bro. You gotta come out."

The Lee family is a big one: 12 kids. They grew up in Pittsburgh's southern neighborhood of Beltzhoover with their mother, Marjorie.

When Paul and Andy talk about their childhood, they smile. When they talk about their teenage years, there's a shift in their demeanor. It was around that time in the late 1980s when crack entered the neighborhood and the people and places in their narrative sound increasingly desperate and neglected.

Even today, the epidemic of drug overdoses, largely reported as a white suburban crisis, is heavily impacting the black community. According to the Centers for Disease Control and Prevention, the drug death rate is increasing the fastest for black people ages 45 to 64. In urban counties nationwide, CDC data shows drug deaths among blacks rose by 41 percent in 2016, compared to deaths among whites rising by 19 percent in the same year.

Wendell "Kaba" Wilson, 48, grew up with the Lee brothers. They played in the street, went to school together and sometimes fought each other, too. As an adult, Kaba struggled with addiction for decades. He now calls Paul his best friend.

Kaba remembers the change in Beltzhoover after crack hit the streets. He had gone to live with his mother in Atlanta and finish high school. He was out of Pittsburgh from 1986 to 1988. When he came back, he was shocked. It was no longer the place he once called "wonderful."

"It was like the life was sucked out of the neighborhood. It was awful."

Kaba remembers asking someone, "What the hell is going on?" They told him it was crack. He asked them, "What the hell is crack?" Kaba was 18. In three years, he would become a crack addict so thin that his mother in Atlanta wouldn't recognize him. Kaba said that when he called out her name in a bus terminal, she fainted when she realized he was her son.

Black men disappearing from their lives was a common occurrence. It happened so often that people didn't question it. People assumed a missing black man was either dead, incarcerated or on drugs. In 2015, the New York Times reported that 1.5 million black men are missing from society largely due to incarceration or death.

In the 1980s, the federal crack statute was passed; it's also known as the 100-to-1 rule. Possessing 5 grams of crack carried the same five-year mandatory minimum sentence as distribution of 500 grams of powder cocaine. There were racial factors at play: Crack was cheaper and largely seen as a drug chosen by black people. Cocaine was seen as a white person's drug and its use occasionally glamorized in the media.

In 2010, Congress passed the Fair Sentencing Act, lessening the disparity in mandatory minimum sentences between crack and cocaine charges. By then, neighborhoods like Beltzhoover had already lost people for decades to the prison system.

Paul and Kaba, though friends when they were children, did not cross paths much while they were using drugs. Kaba said he heard stories that Paul was doing badly and he assumed Paul was dead or incarcerated. Kaba said he figured people assumed that about him, too.

Kaba and Paul essentially disappeared into a cloud of addiction for decades.

Family loss stymied Paul's attempts to shake his addiction. He relapsed in December 2003 when he found out that his twin brother, Peter, had died of a heroin overdose. At the time, Paul had maybe two months clean. He had tried to quit cold turkey.

After the coroner's office called Paul, he walked out of his sister's house in a daze. A man he knew came up and grabbed Paul's hand. He said he was sorry for Paul's loss before walking away. Paul opened up his hand and in it was a crack rock.

"The power of the crack rock... truly interrupted not only my grief but my recovery," Paul said. "It changed my life. That one incident changed my life forever."

Peter wasn't the first brother the Lees had lost suddenly. Paul and Andy's older brother Glen was murdered in Beltzhoover in 1990. When Glen died, the Lee family family lost its breadwinner, because their father wasn't around.

Before Glen was murdered, Andy told Glen that he had made it two years clean. Glen kissed his little brother on the cheek and said, "I am so happy for you. But I can't stop." It was Paul and Andy who introduced Glen to cocaine.

Losing both brothers fueled an addiction Paul couldn't escape.

ACT TWO: Waking Up

Paul, despite being an addict, spurred his younger brother Andy to get clean.

When Andy was still in active addiction, he stole drugs from Paul and ran into the bathroom. Paul pursued, but retreated when he saw the hateful look in Andy's eyes.

"It was in him walking away that I felt hurt and disgusted for I knew what I had done," Andy said, "but I was addicted so I had to have it."

This moment, this shame, pushed Andy to end his two-year addiction. He asked God for help. He went to his first Narcotics Anonymous [NA] meeting the next day and stopped using drugs. He went back to school and got a degree in business administration from Robert Morris University. He had a family and later became a preacher.

Andy remained clean, but he became Paul's enabler and guardian. He'd rescue Paul from getting beat up. He'd keep Paul's money for him. Whenever Paul called, Andy answered.

That's why Paul went to Andy first after running into his daughters' aunt on the street about 14 years ago: "She says, 'Paul, your daughters are coming to Pittsburgh for Thanksgiving.'"

Paul had recently gotten out of jail for drug charges and was getting high again.

Paul's daughters were teenagers. Their mother had moved them to Memphis, Tennessee, away from Paul and Pittsburgh when his oldest was about 5 years old. The girls' mother was in addiction recovery and moved to Memphis to start a new life. She and Paul were never married; they used drugs together when she lived in Pittsburgh.

The day Paul found out his daughters were coming home, he sought Andy out. Andy had Paul's last $300 for safekeeping. Paul was essentially homeless at the time, and Andy would dole out his money to him. They were in a car together.

Paul told Andy, "Man, I've got to buy some clothes. I can't let my daughters see me like this."

Andy started to cry.

Paul asked his brother, "Why are you crying?"

Paul thought to himself, "Damn, my brother is crying" and seconds later, "But, I need that money."

Andy said he didn't want to give Paul the money: "I said, 'No. You need to deal with the reality of who you are.'"

Andy told Paul that he was an embarrassment, that he has shamed their family. Addiction transformed Paul from the "the good kid," the boy who wanted to be a police officer, the son who didn't want to leave his mom's side, to the addict who stole money from his mother on her deathbed. "And now that your kids are coming to see who their dad really is, why put on a charade?" Andy said.

Paul can't remember what he said to Andy, but he got his money and Andy sped off crying. Andy said this is the first time he told Paul the truth. He said, "It was also the moment when I was able to let go." Andy drove away from Paul. He had officially cut himself off from his brother.

With the money, Paul planned to go to Family Dollar to buy underwear, a jacket and jeans. He never made it. Paul ran into a guy who asked him if he wanted to get high.

"Of course, I gave in," Paul said. "And when I seen my daughters, I looked just the way that my brother said I should have looked. Pathetic."

Paul followed his daughters around town. They wouldn't come to visit his side of the family, so he sat in the living rooms of strangers. While visiting, the mother of Paul's children relapsed. Paul smoked crack with her. She rented out her car to a drug dealer. She had been in Pittsburgh three days.

"It was the first time I said to myself, 'Man, you can't do this. You got to get your babies out of here,'" Paul said.

Somehow, Paul convinced his ex to leave Pittsburgh and drugs behind again. Paul said this is how he knows love has incredible power: he wasn't thinking about himself. In his own way, he felt he protected his children.

Before they left for Memphis, Paul was in the car with his daughters. His oldest daughter turned to him and said, "Where do you want to be dropped off, Dad?"

She spat the word at him.

"This is where God kicked in. God literally kicked in. He allowed me to see her. Not what she was exhibiting but what was causing her to exhibit that anger. And I looked through my baby and I said, 'Oh my god.' I started to cry and I said, 'I can't believe what I've done.' It was like I woke up out of a 20-year-old dream. ...I saw her pain that I caused. And I looked at her and I said, 'You will never, ever, ever see me like this again.' That was the last day I used."

It was November 26, 2004. That's his clean-since date.

Paul rebounded in dramatic form after a decades-long addiction.

He earned an associate degree in liberal arts and sciences from the

Community College of Allegheny County [CCAC] in 2008, a bachelor's degree in psychology from Carlow University with a minor in counseling in 2011, and a master's in social work from the University of Pittsburgh in 2014.

Now, he's a therapist and certified social worker in the recovery community. He's won several awards for his academics and work in recovery.

Paul said graduate school almost broke him. The racism he faced in academia was not something he was prepared for. He thought he had overcome the major hurdles in his life by the time he got clean. He's been asked to talk about addiction recovery at regional conferences, but he said he's been asked to avoid discussing racism and systemic oppression when talking about his journey.

That's challenging because it is his experience of being black and male in America that motivates him to stay clean: "The anger, the hurt, was a motivational factor in my recovery," Paul said. Once Paul got clean, he was still black. "That's when it got real."

Paul lives in Sheraden now. When he visits Beltzhoover, people can't believe he has a master's degree. "Getting a master's degree is like going to the moon."

In last decade, Paul has had two more children: Michael, 10, and Grace, 7. Michael's mother, Ashlie, died of a heroin overdose last year. They originally met at a NA meeting. Paul describes his relationship with Ashlie like another addiction—toxic relationships are far stronger than healthy ones. Paul stayed with Ashlie for seven years through her addiction.

"She'd say, 'You're only with me because of Michael,' and that was the truth," Paul said. He wanted Michael to have a mother in his life. He eventually cut the relationship off.

Paul has full custody of Michael and Grace and has taken care of them while finishing his degrees. Last summer, he was at the mall with his children and grandson when he got a call from Ashlie's mother. She was in the hospital. She wasn't going to make it.

"I told Michael right there in the mall," he said. "I took them to see her in the hospital. She was unconscious… Overdose. I wanted him to at least see her. That was the last time. She passed away. 28. She didn't get a chance really to live."

Paul tells his story in group therapy to help those with substance abuse disorder understand the importance of decision-making. "I want to give them an out-of-the-box view of how serious your decisions are."

Nine years ago, Kaba was sitting in the Allegheny County Jail when Paul Lee appeared on the TV screen. He couldn't believe it. It was a commercial for CCAC. He thought to himself, "That can't be Paul. The Paul I know is messed up."

"That was kind of a hope shot for me when I got clean," Kaba said.

Kaba was approaching 40 and still smoking crack, still getting arrested over and over. He was transferred from the jail to Renewal, a rehabilitation center in Downtown Pittsburgh. He went to a NA meeting and there was Paul. He and Paul continued to go to meetings together.

They forged a true friendship after all those years of using. They supported each other. Paul even took Kaba to take his driving license test. They helped each other move and call each other when things aren't going so well, when recovery is hardest. Kaba said Paul is always with his kids and he watches how patiently he talks to them. He doesn't yell.

Paul leans down and whispers to his children, and Kaba just thinks, "Wow, man."

Andy can't believe what Paul has become either.

"I can't tell you how proud of him I am, to just see the accomplishments," Andy said.

Paul's children are now his priority. He does the cooking, cleaning and homework patrol. Michael just got into Pittsburgh CAPA, the district's creative and performing arts magnet.

"As an educated man, I make sure that education is first for them. So, as soon as they come home, homework's done first."

For his youngest children, Paul has been an anchor, a man they have seen and trusted every day of their lives. For him to disappear is unthinkable, out of character. They've never met the man who lived on the street, was arrested and hid the truth from his family. And while Paul has a community, multiple degrees and a vocation that keeps him grounded, it is because of Michael and Grace that he can never disappear again.

The Squonk of Beltzhoover

ALMAH LAVON RICE

Long before I moved to Pennsylvania, I knew to keep ears peeled for the sound of the squonk, seldom-seen and misunderstood monster of the region. According to its (pseudo)scientific name, *Lacrimacorpus dissolvens*, it sounds like:

Tear.

Body.

Dissolve.

Covered with warts, it is known for its weeping most of all. If you corner a squonk, you will be confronted with nothing but a puddle of tears and bubbles at your feet. Your catch is melancholy and rumor.

So when I moved in with my partner, across from a wall of trees in the South Hills of Pittsburgh, I knew not to expect more than the sound of anonymous weeping roaming through the leaves. Our house faces McKinley Park, the jewel of Beltzhoover. Although the park is currently undergoing revitalization, including the installation of a plaza and pavilion, I treasure McKinley Park for its human-scarce secrets most of all. The wild turkey pirouetting alone in the clearing. The woodpecker splitting the morning in two. The coyote yips and cries. The trio of deer that cross the street at twilight, headed to the abandoned house a few steps from ours. I joke with my partner that the deer go over there to hold séances. More than anything, I cherish the hush of deep dark that falls over the park at night.

And then the sounds begin.

Sometimes it's just the dogs. I don't know where they live, exactly, but you can hear them casting lassos of barks to catch their kin. *Here I am here I am here I am,* they seem to be calling all together, all at once.

Sometimes it's those coyotes. They tend to speak long after the dogs have gone to bed. The coyotes would rather talk to the moon anyway.

Sometimes—I dread these sometimes—it's a domestic fight that has spilled out into the street. My body is rapt, waiting for thunderclap. I keep peeking out of the window, wondering if what I will see will prompt me to act beyond witness.

Most of the time, though, the night trees across the street breathe out quiet. It's against this backdrop that I kiss my partner good night and tuck into my bedside book while she descends into dreamland. After a while, I turn off the light and follow her.

One night I am barely asleep. Then I am very awake. Do I hear a woman crying for help? It's strange and percussive. Almost otherworldly. But it has to be a woman in distress. What else could it be? I peer on to the dark street and see nothing illuminating. I return to bed and rouse my partner: "Do you hear that? What is it?" She mumbles something, and it becomes apparent to me that if I want to figure this out now, I'll have to figure it out alone.

Somehow I get lucky hunting the wilds of Google. I find recordings of what has been called "the vixen's scream" (although male foxes are known to use the same vocalization), and the mystery appears to be put to bed. So I have been eavesdropping on a mating call. Later that morning, I update my now more alert partner: our neighbor wasn't being slaughtered—it was a fox lookin' for love!

Tear. Body. Dissolve. It's not until more nights of these calls, and months pass, that it occurs to me that I am assuming that these are the sounds of a fox being ripped apart by desire. Sure, YouTube is replete with fox calls that sound just like what I heard on those clear, cold nights. But I have never laid eyes on these amorous foxes. I've seen more puddles that the feral cats drink from than I have seen foxes.

Crafton-Ingram

LISA PICKETT

Running Parallel.

_____

Steuben Street.

_____

Ingram Avenue.

_____

Don't matter— cause they both lead to the little, lost, lonely bold legged brown skin girl skipping down Maxwell Street. Ingram Ave. Negley Ave. Stotz Ave. Walsh Road.

The whisper of that mysterious mesmerizing Wooden Park calling her name finds her feet planted firmly in its crisp bright green grass gasping for the next calm breeze to brush across her face. Swinging, swaying, swiftly. Pump. Push. Pull. Higher and higher. Adrenaline taking the lead. Leaping. Letting go.

Flying through the trauma…the tears. Letting go….Letting go… letting go. Bam. Solid landing on the foundation of familiarity.

Grinning as the little splinters filled with laughter prance on her fingers

dancing to meet the beat of the dirty leather softball soaring high in the sky as it greets

the call of the sun's mitt catching the exhilaration of the next C.I.T. championship.

She inhales itching for the calm of the Crafton pool to wash away those childhood insecurities.

Splish. Splash. Strawberry Shortcake Ice Cream Bars. Wet swimsuits. $2 white lawn chairs. French fries. Cold Pepsi cans. Bare toes tickled by the brown ants sneaking by.

Tip toeing past the yellow jacket guarding the cross walk as she skips over Steuben Street to Ingram Days. Holding tight to a bit of togetherness and the crunch of that bright, red, shiny candy apple sticking to her palm.

Crafton Celebrates pulls her away and secretly hands her the last sweet fried funnel cake with vanilla ice cream on top… just before the mesmerizing lights fire, twist, and whirl in the air. Crack. Bang Bang. Whistle. Boom!

Silence.

Calm.

There it is…

Peace gliding through the air to kiss the promenade of beautiful white Cherry Trees reigning royally over Steuben street as they serenade her with special soft silly spectacular sprinkles of childhood.

There they go marching down Ingram avenue dressed as little monsters and witches in the annual Halloween Parade. Prancing back on over to Resurrection Sunday hunting for those Ingram Park golden Easter eggs.

Shhhhhh….listen…across the way…down past Kentucky Fried Chicken and Payless….her Granddad LeRoy is calling her name as the scent of his Mug Shots Cafe floating fried fish sandwich lands right on her nose. Grandma's glance. Aunt Di Di's grin. Cousin Chuck's chuckle. Eyes watching God.

The sun sets as the night takes hold.

It's time to come back little brown girl. Be sure to pull the screen door tight. No need to lock the front door. It's time for B.E.D. Rest. Recover. Heal. Cause it's Crafton. It's Ingram. It's where your childhood sleeps safely.

Thorn Street

SHANNON SANKEY

from We Ran Rapturous (The Atlas Review)

For groceries, we drive
to the good part of town,
where shopkeepers lock their doors at us.
Through window glass, sacks
of coffee beans and hanging scarves
catch evening light like wet treasures
on the soft tongue of the sea.
We push past like a rogue wave,
where long white porches
stay warm as ripe oranges,
where linen curtains glow soft on clean bay windows,
where a boy on a skateboard doesn't know yet
that we won't turn
into a driveway
—and waits.

On Steps

SHANNON SANKEY

from We Ran Rapturous (The Atlas Review)

I visit my mother
at her husband's house
and we wait for the harvest moon
on her porch steps.

In the suburbs,
the ferns are fresh
and fragrant, the wind white and wet.

We are still and silent.
We offer up our faces
like paper plates.
When we lived together
as girls, we were quick.

We carried bags
up city steps
in trips and shifts,
up from yellow brick
and trolley tracks,
out of closing markets
and six-pack pubs.

We climbed to small dark house after small dark
house, all those years.
We were strong, lifting our gallons of milk,

and we spoke the whole way,
soft, with sweet spring
water in our throats.

The Suburbs Are Stunned

BOWIE ROWAN

In 1959, less than ten miles outside the city of Pittsburgh, a high school was built like a college campus. Comprised of eight buildings, each one housed different subjects and homerooms for every grade level. Bethel Park Senior High School was meant to serve additionally as a campus for the Community College of Allegheny County. So, in some ways, the campus makes sense then, I think. But mostly, an open high school campus in Western Pennsylvania, with its harsh winters—even harsher before the last several decades of global warming—now seems like a practice in teenage torture.

My mother and father went to Bethel Park Senior High School. But they were four years apart. They never shared snowy walks between buildings one and eight—their hair turning into icicles in the cold after swim class—or held hands while cutting through every building across campus for respite from the cold. Despite the ice and snow, there were advantages to the campus for a troubled kid like my mom. An open campus meant there were secret spots behind buildings to make out with boys and smoke cigarettes and weed before the bell rang.

An open, mostly unguarded campus made it easy for a kid to skip class. By my senior year at Bethel Park Senior High School, I walked off campus unbothered before I finished my

classes for the day at least once a week. But an open campus also made it easy for anyone, from anywhere, to walk onto it and into classrooms as well, without ever being noticed.

*

The first time I heard that someone died from a gunshot was in 1997. I was ten. Ennis Cosby, Bill Cosby's son, was murdered in Los Angeles during a failed robbery attempt. Despite what we all know about Bill Cosby now in 2020, all I knew or cared about then was that somebody's son was dead. It was difficult for me to comprehend, but eventually, I made sense of it. At ten, I already knew, death would come for me someday too.

Before I saw the gruesome news coverage of Ennis Cosby's death— his bloody body on the side of the road showed on a TV screen on repeat—my only real understanding of what could cause death was old age or sickness. In 1997, I had already seen and experienced various kinds of violence as a young girl, but not the kind that killed you—even if you felt like it might.

Before the death of Ennis Cosby, when I thought of guns, I saw the slack jaws of deer, their blank stares gnawing at me from the bed of a neighbor's pickup truck. As a girl, I fed apples to the deer that visited us in our small backyard. Mom put out salt blocks for them in the summer, though now I'm uncertain why. My family didn't own guns nor did anyone have the financial luxury or time to go hunting. I can only assume she wanted to attract them so I could give them apples and ensure they were fed.

One night, when I couldn't sleep, I stumbled to the kitchen in the dark, filling a glass with water before almost dropping it. Through the window above the sink, a deer's watery gaze stared back at me. I could feel its animal heat so close behind that flimsy window screen. We looked at each other for longer than I'd ever looked at another animal, human or not. I felt a sense of recognition I hadn't yet felt with any human in my life.

Ever since I was a girl, I have always wondered, why would anyone want to kill a creature as beautiful as this?

———————————

It's 1999 when I cover my bedroom walls with images of the band NSYNC and high school seniors Eric Harris and Dylan Klebold murder twelve students and one teacher at Columbine High School in Colorado. When I see the news, I can't help but think that, despite the trench coats, they look a lot like my older brother. Tall, skinny, white, male, teenager. It scares me. So do the new drills at school. The ones where we huddle together in the far end of the room after the teacher locks the door and we wait, trying not to imagine a skinny boy with a gun blasting down the classroom door before murdering us all.

I am twelve and in school at Independence Middle School on a small hill just next to the high school when Eric Harris and Dylan Klebold kill their fellow students and teacher at Columbine. My brother is a sophomore at Bethel Park Senior High School then. He is a student on an open campus. I try not to think of everything that could happen to him.

After Columbine, I take a break from the news to focus on the more manageable and mundane daily dramas of my almost-teen life. Or perhaps my parents stopped letting me watch the news, though that level of surveillance from them when I was a tween is unlikely. More likely, is this: the news was so overwhelming, I watched it, and often, but now, I remember little after Columbine because I blocked it out.

Richard Baumhammers was born in Pittsburgh, Pennsylvania in 1965, only two years after the birth of my mother. Like Richard, my mother spent her early years in a small house in Mount Lebanon, even closer to the city of Pittsburgh, than Bethel Park. A convenient neighborhood for those who lived and worked in the city like Richard's parents did, both of them faculty members at the University of Pittsburgh's School of Dental Medicine.

My mother's father was a trolley car driver. Eventually, my family moved to a house in Bethel Park on the trolley line because it was cheaper and more convenient for my grandfather's job. Richard spent high school at Mount Lebanon, a rival of the Bethel Park Blackhawks, before going off to college and then law school while my mother became a pregnant teen divorced from my brother's abusive biological father before she could legally drink.

Richard became an immigration lawyer and returned to Pittsburgh in the late 90s. He was having some problems. Only later would his father admit that he'd seen signs since his son was a boy.

Whenever Richard leaves the psychiatric hospital where he was committed, he returns to his parents' home in Mount Lebanon. He decides to travel, moving to Latvia where he stays close to where his grandparents once lived in the 1930s.

Before his travels, he'd never really been in trouble before.

It's 1999, the same year as the Columbine shooting and me covering my room with images of NSYNC ripped from magazines, when Richard's arrested for assaulting a woman in Paris because he believed her to be Jewish. He's detained for a short period of time before leaving for Spain.

A year later, after we all survived the turn of the millennium, Richard's back in Pittsburgh when he buys a Smith & Wesson .357 Magnum revolver just south of the city.

First, he shoots and kills his parents' friend and neighbor of more than 30 years before setting her house on fire. She is Jewish.

Traveling a little north of Mount Lebanon in his Jeep, Richard shoots through the windows of a synagogue before murdering a 31-year-old man shopping for groceries at the local India Grocers. The store manager survives the shooting, dying later of complications at the age of 32.

Moving closer to the city, in the town of Carnegie, Richard shoots through another synagogue's windows. Continuing on, he drives west of Pittsburgh to a town not far from the airport before shooting and killing a young restaurant manager and a cook in front of customers at a Chinese restaurant.

Richard continues.

Traveling further down the Ohio River, away from the city, he finds his final victim: a 22-year-old Black man who happens to be working out in a karate school.

Like so many of these stories, a manifesto is later found in Richard's home in Mount Lebanon. It is a familiar and untrue story. European Americans are being outnumbered.

Minorities and immigrants are the problem. A website is also discovered where Richard had clearly, and publicly, stated his racist, xenophobic beliefs.

Here are the facts: Richard was arrested for physically assaulting a woman after believing she was Jewish. Richard had a documented history of mental illness. Richard was still able to buy a gun.

"Shootings Leave Pittsburgh Suburbs Stunned" a *New York Times* article reports in April of 2000 just after Richard Baumhammers went on his shooting spree through three counties surrounding the city of Pittsburgh. Only a few months before this, a Black man was charged for racially motivated killings in the neighborhood of Wilkinsburg.

The more I read, the more I am overwhelmed by the number of shootings during the spring of 2000 alone, not only in Pittsburgh, but across the United States.

Perhaps I don't remember Baumhammers' spree in particular because its shock was absorbed by a sea of national violence, delusion, and cruelty. Perhaps I don't remember because I couldn't after the particular kind of contact I first felt with chance and death in the wake of Ennis Cosby's murder.

Eighteen years later in October 2018, another *New York Times* headline reads: "Quiet Day at a Pittsburgh Synagogue Became a Battle to Survive."

The deadliest attack ever committed on the Jewish community in the United States is in the neighborhood of Squirrel Hill in the city of Pittsburgh where I was born. Shortly before the massacre, two independent reports showed a peak in anti-semitic activity online, similar to the rises reported surrounding the 2016 presidential election.

The suspect: another white man obsessed with the alt-right who had a history of posting hateful beliefs publicly online.

Like Richard Baumhammers, Robert Gregory Bowers, the 2018 Squirrel Hill shooter, lived in a suburb of Pittsburgh just south of the city. Baldwin: a township only a little east of Mount Lebanon and Bethel Park.

Baldwin High School being where Bowers went to school before dropping out and where I took my SATs for the second time during my senior year of high school.

Baldwin being where Bowers' neighbors described him as a ghost.

In 1959, the year Bethel Park Senior High School was built, I wonder if the architect considered the possibility of a lone gunman walking onto campus, spraying the inside of buildings one through eight with bullets while students hid inside classrooms or attempted to flee.

School shootings have been reported since the 18th century. There is a seemingly endless list of them labeled "List of School Shootings" organized by century on Wikipedia. A law professor shot by a student in 1840 in Charlottesville, Virginia. A father who shot a schoolmaster to death after the schoolmaster strangled his son to death for killing his tame sparrow. Many more killings of teachers by students and parents and vice versa. The death of two students by gunfire at a school dance in Plain Dealing, Louisiana in 1893. 1904 in Chicago, Illinois, the murder of a 16-year-old boy by another boy after fighting over a girl. An 11-year-old student in Trinidad, Colorado in 1909 who accidentally killed his teacher while on a school trip. The rape and murder of a 19-year-old female teacher in 1916 in Bemidji, Minnesota. The killer just walked right into the school while the teacher was alone.

The list goes on and on. The number of deaths and injuries per shooting rising through the years until we see 18 dead in Austin, Texas in 1966 when an engineering student shot bullets from the observation deck of the Main Building tower at the University of Texas at Austin. Like Richard Baumhammers of Pittsburgh, Charles Whitman had a documented history of violence and mental illness.

The University of Texas tower shooting was the most fatal campus shooting until 2007 when at Virginia Tech, another student shot and killed more than 30 students and staff. Like Robert Gregory Bowers of Baldwin, Seung-Hui Cho was described as quiet, someone you might barely notice if it weren't for their perceived lonesomeness.

I am struck by how as the years pass, the documented school shootings seem to move from personal to impersonal rage. From eye for an eye revenge to shootings growing larger in scale motivated by racism, sexism, xenophobia, and mental illness.

Today, in 2020, as I traverse public spaces throughout the world, I often fail to subdue my anxiety whenever I hear an unexpected loud noise or I pass an agitated man in the movie theater or grocery store because all I can think is *Gun. Gun, gun, gun.*

Over the last handful of years, when one of my students has become demonstrably angry (they have all been male and white), by slamming the door or banging the desk as they walk out of my office when I tell them something they don't want to hear (*you're failing, you're tardy every day, you plagiarized, I discovered you forged government documents to get out of class*), all I can think is *Gun. Gun, gun, gun.* I go to bed at night running through my head how I might protect my other students if one of these boys came to class with a gun. I feel insane, overly sensitive, dramatic, but am I?

I'm a college senior at the University of Pittsburgh in 2009 when my writing professor shows a video in class to demonstrate something important about point of view, how depending on when and how you learn information, your perspective of a character or narrator will change. The video she shows us is of a man giving a tour of his apartment. It's innocuous and boring on first view. When she reveals to us that the man is George Sodini, I feel sick, and another student gets up quickly before leaving the room.

Only a few months before, Sodini shot and killed three people in an LA Fitness outside of Pittsburgh, injuring nine others. The daughter of my mother's boss was one of the victims. Not long before this, I was at her wedding where I remember her vividly, smiling in her ornate sari. Luckily, she survived, but I would hear reports over the next year from afar after I moved to San Francisco for my first job post-graduation. She was having trouble leaving the house.

Everywhere I went in San Francisco, I imagined a man pulling out a gun. Sodini had a history of posting hate speech online about women, yet he was still able to purchase a weapon.

In 2009, when my classmate came back into the room, she apologized before saying quietly, "I'm sorry, but I had to leave. I was one of the women he shot."

Shortly after I graduate from college, I vote to keep Bethel Park Senior High School an open campus. I'm not totally certain I can explain why, but I'd like to try. Despite my increasing fear of guns since I was a kid, voting for tax dollars to be used to tear down a perfectly functioning school and replace it with another felt like waste and also like failure. It made me angry. Angry to know that kids would be locked away in a new school that would be more like a prison. Angry that they wouldn't have the same choice and freedom to learn and make mistakes by skipping class or making out and smoking weed behind building five. Maybe they'd be safer in some ways, I argued with myself, but ultimately, a new school could only protect them from the realities and choices that lay ahead for so long. They would still leave school for the parking lot or to catch the bus. They would still go to the movies and the mall.

I voted for the campus to remain because nowhere is fully safe. What if our tax dollars were used to aid in enacting more gun control efforts and offering mental health services to those in need instead? Bethel Park Senior High School was colloquially called Heroin High by the time I graduated in 2005. In fact, the boy who sat in front of me in homeroom every day for years died of an overdose shortly before we were meant to graduate. My brother's best friend passed a few years later after first encountering heroin from another suburban high schooler.

This was the reality. The reality we all knew as teenagers, even if adults didn't like to talk to us directly about it as we locked doors and hid behind desks on the far side of the classroom during drills, holding our breath.

The unspoken reality we lived with every day was this: If someone wanted to shoot a bunch of us at school badly enough, campus or not, they would find a way.

When I voted from the cubicle of my first after-college editorial assistant job in San Francisco, I felt defeated and depressed before I even knew the verdict. I wasn't surprised when I received an email letting me know that I lost. My high school campus was torn down and one massive building took its place. I've driven by, and just like I thought, it looks like a prison. I like to think that the students are safer than my brother and I were in the late 90s and early 2000s, but I don't really believe this. I see the new school only as a Band-Aid on a larger cultural problem that has been hemorrhaging for decades.

Last year, shortly after I finished graduate school, I was bartending in the wealthiest municipality of Pennsylvania, a suburb called Fox Chapel. It was early that day and our shift had only just begun when one of the servers began talking about a shooting at a Walmart in El Paso, TX. More than 20 people were killed and more than 20 were injured.

"This is why my brother refuses to take his kids to any large stores," I say. "He feels guilty, but he buys everything on Amazon because he's so afraid of being at the wrong place at the wrong time."

"You can't live like that," one of the chefs says leaning against the bar. The manager turns down the lights before customers arrive, leaving the room as soon as the gun and murder talk begin.

"This is what they want," the server says. He's smiling shyly like he often does when he's about to make what he thinks is a profound point. His cheeks are round and covered in freckles. He pulls at the strings on his brown apron. "Division. Isolation. That's how they gain control."

It's unclear who the "they" is that he's referring to. I'm uncertain he even knows, but I understand his meaning. There is always someone who profits from hatred and violence. All you have to do is follow wherever the trail of money takes you.

When one of the other servers walks by the bar, the small group standing around me as I cut lemon and lime garnishes grows quiet like it always does when he's around. There has been an ongoing joke since we all opened the restaurant together a few months before that he'll be the one to shoot us all. He's of course young, white, male, quiet, easily agitated. I feel guilty every time I laugh when someone says it. I laugh only because letting myself come into contact with my real fear feels far too overwhelming for conversation with coworkers, most of whom I'm hoping I won't see again as soon as I find another job.

I feel bad for the server we all fear, but I'm also suspicious. We aren't necessarily wrong for feeling afraid of him. Months before during an early training, he asked me for my number so he could take me out for coffee. I gave it to him, though I wasn't completely sure I wanted to spend time alone with him. We hadn't talked much, so I was unsure of his intentions. I was too afraid to reject him outright, especially around new coworkers. When he texted me, I told him I was too busy that week, but we should try again for the following. He never texted back or talked directly to me again, except for once, in the middle of a rush, he asked if I took tranquilizers. Busy and confused, I asked him what he meant. "I don't know how you stay so calm," he said, unexpectedly looking me in the eye before rushing away.

Shortly after that day, I saw him sleeping face down at a table in the gas station across the street from the bar. I felt soft towards him before becoming afraid. I can't explain why, but seeing him like that didn't evoke sustained pity or compassion in me, though I thought it should. After that moment, I began to be extra aware and kind to him whenever he needed something from me at the bar. I feel absurd admitting it, but if I'm honest, the thought often passed through my mind that maybe if he did decide to shoot us all, he would take pity on me if I could only get him to look me in the eye. Time would slow down, and for a moment, the world would feel a little safer and more beautiful like it did all those years ago when I caught the gaze of that deer through the kitchen window in the middle of the night.

He will look at me and I will look at him. And we will see together what is impossible to see when you're living inside a prison of fear and rage and loneliness. We will see in each other what is always there but too often goes unseen: We are beautiful, vulnerable creatures capable of equanimity, understanding, and love. Then we will follow a question until we feel the weight of the truth of our connectedness, no matter how much we may try to deny it through differing identities, ideologies, hate, and violence.

The question where we will meet each other fully for the first time in mutual frailty and humility will be this: Why would anyone want to kill a creature as beautiful as us?

Contributors

Kelly Lorraine Andrews' poems have appeared in *Dream Pop Journal*, *Ghost Proposal*, *Ninth Letter*, *PANK*, and *Prick of the Spindle*, among others. She is the author of five chapbooks, including *Sonnets in Which the Speaker Is on Display* (Stranded Oak Press, 2019), *The Fear Archives* (Two of Cups Press, 2017), and *My Body Is a Poem I Can't Stop Writing* (Porkbelly Press 2017). She received her MFA in poetry from the University of Pittsburgh, and she edits the online journal *Pretty Owl Poetry*. Additional information about her publications, along with a slideshow of her cats, can be found at kellyandrewspoetry.com.

Cameron Barnett is the author of *The Drowning Boy's Guide to Water*, winner of the 2017 Rising Writer Contest and a finalist for an NAACP Image Award. He is the recipient of a 2019 Investing in Professional Artists Grant Program and winner of the 2019 Carol R. Brown Creative Achievement Award for Emerging Artist, a partnership of the Pittsburgh Foundation and the Heinz Endowments. Cameron is an editor for *Pittsburgh Poetry Journal* and works as a teacher in the Oakland neighborhood of Pittsburgh. His work explores the complexity of race and the body for Black people in today's America.

Brian Broome is an instructor and fellow at the University of Pittsburgh. His book *Punch Me Up to the Gods* will be published in 2021. More at: brianbroome.me

Jim Daniels is the author of many books of poems, including, most recently, *Rowing Inland* and *Street Calligraphy*. His sixth book of fiction, *The Perp Walk*, was published by Michigan State University Press in 2019, along with the anthology he edited with M.L. Liebler, *RESPECT: The Poetry of Detroit Music*. He lives in Pittsburgh, where he has been teaching at Carnegie Mellon University since 1981.

Tuhin Das is a Bengali poet currently living in the U.S. He comes from Barishal, a city in south-central Bangladesh. He was involved in the Little Magazine Movement and edited several literary magazines; he has had poetry criticism articles, short stories, and opinion columns broadly published in the last twenty years in Bangladesh and West Bengal, India. He is the author of eight poetry books in his native language. He is considered by critics as a significant poet of Generation Zero, who began publishing contemporary Bangladeshi literature in 2000. His life was deeply impacted by groups who limit freedom of expression. Carnegie Mellon University invited him to Pittsburgh, PA as a visiting scholar, and City of Asylum invited him to join their writer sanctuary program. He left his home country, Bangladesh, in 2016. Das' work appeared in *The Logue Project's Home Language, Words Without Borders, The Bare Life Review, Immigrant Report, The Offing,* and *Epiphany.* His poetry book *Exile Poems* is forthcoming from Bridge & Tunnel Books.

Corinne Duval is originally from Cleveland and currently resides in Pittsburgh. She is a graduate of Chatham University with a BA in English Literature and Cultural Studies.

Sherrie Flick is the author of a novel and two short story collections. Her nonfiction appears in *Ploughshares, The Wall Street Journal, Creative Nonfiction,* and *Pittsburgh Magazine.* She has received fellowships from Pennsylvania Council on the Arts, Sewanee Writers' Conference, and Atlantic Center for the Arts. She served as series editor for *The Best Small Fictions 2018* and is co-editor for the anthology *Flash Fiction America,* forthcoming from W.W. Norton in 2022.

Richard L. Gegick is the author of the poetry collection *Greasy Handshakes* from WPA Press. His poetry and short stories have appeared in *Burrow Press Review, Chiron Review,* Barrelhouse, *Edison Literary Review* among many others. Originally from Trafford, PA, he lives in the Manchester neighborhood of Pittsburgh and waits tables for a living.

Mike Good lives in Wilkinsburg and serves as managing editor of Autumn House Press. His recent poetry and book reviews can be found in or are forthcoming at *december, The Carolina Quarterly, Five Points, Forklift, OH, Full Stop, The Georgia Review, Pleiades, Salamander, Spillway, SOFTBLOW,* and elsewhere. His work has received support from the Sewanee Writers' Conference and The Sun, and he holds an MFA from Hollins University.

Vince Guerrieri is a journalist and author who spent his salad days as a reporter and sports copy editor for the *Pittsburgh Tribune-Review.* He's since written about Southwestern Pennsylvania for *CityLab* and *Smithsonian*. You can find him on Twitter at @vinceguerrieri or on his website, www. vinceguerrieri.com

Brittany Hailer is a freelance reporter and educator based in Pittsburgh, Pennsylvania. She reports on mental health, addiction and incarceration. In 2019, she was nominated for the Sally Kalson Courage in Journalism Fund award for her reporting on the mental health effects of active shooter trainings in public schools. For her stories of people affected by the opioid epidemic, she received a 2019 Golden Quill Award from the Press Club of Western Pennsylvania and a Robert L. Vann Award of Excellence for investigative/enterprise reporting from the Pittsburgh Black Media Federation. In 2018, Brittany was selected to be a Justice Reporting Fellow as part of the John Jay/Langeloth Foundation Fellowship on "Reinventing Solitary Confinement." Her work has been funded by the Pittsburgh Foundation and Staunton Family Farm Foundation. Her memoir and poetry collection *Animal You'll Surely Become* was published by Tolsun Books in 2018, which has gone into its second printing. The paperback edition features additional prose and poetry and has been one of Tolsun Books bestsellers. Brittany has taught creative writing classes at the Allegheny County Jail and Sojourner House as part of Chatham's Words Without Walls program and now teaches creative writing and journalism at the University of Pittsburgh. She graduated with a master's in fine arts from Chatham University. Her work as appeared in NPR, *Fairy Tale Review*, *Hobart*, *Barrelhouse*, and elsewhere."

Lori Jakiela is the author of the memoir *Belief Is Its Own Kind of Truth*, *Maybe* (Autumn House 2nd edition, 2019), which received the Saroyan Prize for International Literature from Stanford University. She is the author of two other memoirs—*Miss New York Has Everything* and *The Bridge to Take When Things Get Serious*, as well as a poetry collection, *Spot the Terrorist*, and an essay collection, *Portrait of the Artist as a Bingo Worker*. Her work has been published in the *New York Times*, the *Washington Post*, the *Chicago Tribune*, the *Pittsburgh Post-Gazette*, *The Rumpus*, *Brevity*, *Vol. 1 Brooklyn* and elsewhere. She lives in Trafford, PA with her husband, the writer Dave Newman, and their children.

Lisa L. Kirchner is the author of the critically-acclaimed *Hello American Lady Creature: What I Learned as a Woman in Qatar* (Greenpoint Press).

Most recently, her essay, "Would My Heart Survive Donald Trump?" appeared in *Fury: Women's Lived Experiences During the Trump Era* (Pact Press, 2020). Other writing has appeared in the *New York Times*, the *Washington Post*, and *Salon*, among others. She hosts a monthly storytelling show with Keep St. Pete Lit in Florida, and just finished filming her first production, *My Dinner with Steve*. Follow her on Twitter, @lisalkirchner.

Rachel Mennies is the author of the poetry collections *The Naomi Letters*, forthcoming in 2021 from BOA Editions; *The Glad Hand of God Points Backwards*, the 2014 winner of the Walt McDonald First-Book Prize in Poetry at Texas Tech University Press and finalist for a National Jewish Book Award; and *No Silence in the Fields*, a chapbook from Blue Hour Press. Her poetry and essays have recently appeared at *The Believer, Kenyon Review, American Poetry Review, The Millions, The Poetry Foundation, LitHub*, and numerous other outlets. After living in beloved Pittsburgh for nearly a decade, she moved to Chicago in 2018, where she works as a freelance writer and editor.

Dave Newman is the author of seven books, including the novel *East Pittsburgh Downlow* (J.New Books, 2019), and the collection *The Slaughterhouse Poems* (White Gorilla Press, 2013), named one of the best books of the year by *L Magazine*. A graduate of the writing program at Pitt-Greensburg, and winner of numerous awards, including the Andre Dubus Novella Prize, Newman has published poems, stories, and essays in more than 100 magazines and journals both in the United States and abroad. He lives in Trafford, PA, the last town in the Electric Valley, with his wife, the writer Lori Jakiela, and their two children. He works in medical research, serving elders.

Dr. Lisa Pickett is a Pittsburgh native who is a National Board-Certified educator currently serving as the English Department Instructional Team Leader at the Pittsburgh School for the Creative and Performing Arts. She is the Founder/CEO of L Education Consulting and the Founder/CEO of an online boutique entitled L Apparel and Print Creations. Her creative work has been featured in the literary anthology *Tender* and her academic research in the national journal *Urban Review*.

A native of Johnstown, Pennsylvania, **Shannon Reed** has lived in suburban Pittsburgh since 2012. She is a Lecturer in the Creative Writing program at the University of Pittsburgh, where she also earned her MFA in Creative Writing: Fiction. Shannon is the author of *Why Did I Get a B? And Other Mysteries We're Discussing in the Faculty Lounge*, a work of memoir and humor about her twenty-year teaching career. Her work also frequently appears in the *New Yorker* and *McSweeney's Internet Tendency*, and she has contributed to the *Paris Review*, the *Washington Post, Slate,* the *Georgia Review*, and many other venues. www.shannonreed.org

Almah LaVon Rice is a writer, mixed media mail artist, gift economist, and fairy marsh monster living in Pittsburgh with her flamingo wife. She writes creative nonfiction and weird fiction in the key of AfroSurreal. Her work has appeared in *Black from the Future: A Collection of Black Speculative Writing* (BLF Press), *Queer Magic: Power Beyond Boundaries* (Mystic Productions Press), as well as *TENDER a literary anthology and book of spells: evidence* (These Black Midwives), a bouquet of poetry, prose, and visual art by Black womxn and femmes in Pittsburgh. She's at work on a speculative memoir, an excerpt of which is forthcoming in *The Louisville Anthology* (Belt Publishing).

Bowie Rowan is a writer and multimedia artist. Their work has appeared at *Joyland, Kenyon Review Online, Los Angeles Review,* and *PANK*, among others. Most recently, their audio essay, "How to Survive a Fire," was recognized by the *Missouri Review*'s Miller Audio Prize. Currently, they're at work on their first novel.

Cedric Rudolph is a middle school teacher, editor, and writer. He is a founding editor at *Beautiful Cadaver*, which publishes social justice-themed anthologies and stages theatrical performances. In May 2018, he received his Poetry MFA from Chatham University. His poetry is published in *Christianity and Literature Journal, The Laurel Review,* and *The Sante Fe Literary Review*.

Shannon Sankey is the author of *We Ran Rapturous* (The Atlas Review, 2019). Her poems have appeared at Poets.org, *Best New Poets 2019, Glass: A Journal of Poetry, the minnesota review, Black Warrior Review, Puerto del Sol,* and elsewhere. She is the recipient of a 2017 Academy of American Poets Prize and a 2019 SAFTA residency. She holds an MFA from Chatham University, where she was the Whitford Fellow. She is the founder of Stranded Oak Press. www.shannonsankey.com / @shansankey

Ed Simon is a staff writer for *The Millions* and an editor for *Berfrois*. His writing has appeared in the *New York Times*, the *Atlantic*, the *Paris Review Daily*, and the *Washington Post*, among others. The author of several books, his most recent collection was *Printed in Utopia: The Renaissance's Radicalism*. Belt Publishing will be releasing his *An Alternative History of Pittsburgh* in the spring of 2021.

Arunava Sinha is a noted Indian translator of Bengali literature. He was born and raised in Kolkata. Over fifty of his translations have been published so far. Sinha is an Associate Professor of Creative Writing, at Ashoka University, in New Delhi.

Jason Vrabel is a writer, educator and community development professional. Recently, he has written about housing, eviction and displacement for *PublicSource, Shelterforce Magazine*, the Pittsburgh Foundation and other publications. He was awarded an Investing in Professional Artists grant from the Pittsburgh Foundation and the Heinz Endowments, and was a 2019 Writers Fellow at Creative Nonfiction. He lives in Pittsburgh.

Matthew Wallenstein has a weekly column in the *Pittsburgh Current*. He is the author of the books *Buckteeth* (2020) and *Tiny Alms* (2017). His work has been published by the university of Maine Farmington, Euphony, Albany poets, and others. He lives in Braddock, Pennsylvania.

Alona Williams is a 2020 graduate of Chatham University. She has a BFA in Creative Writing with a Minor in Music. She participated in the Winter Tangerine's Winter 2018 workshop, and has been published in *1839 Magazine, The Minor Bird*, MoonStone Art's Center's journal *Philadelphia Says: Resisting Arrest*, and *TENDER a literary anthology and book of spells: evidence*. Her preferred genre is poetry.

Acknowledgments

Many thanks to Anne Trubek for your patience and continued support, and to Dan Crissman for the thoughtful edits. Thank you to Alex Maihoefer, Alex Nowalk, Liz Morrissey, and Jenna Palmerini, my writing group that always meets off the clock, for the help reading submissions. Additional thanks to TC Jones, Deesha Philyaw, Sarah Shotland, Christine Stroud, and Adlai Yeomans for helping with outreach. Finally, to everyone at Belt Publishing for giving me the opportunity to curate the work of so many great writers in one volume.